The Beverly Hillbillies

→The Beverly Hillbillies←

Stephen Cox

HarperPerennial

A Division Of HarperCollins*Publishers*

FIRST EDITION

Designed by Laura Hough

Library of Congress Cataloging-in-Publication Data
Cox, Stephen, 1966–
    The Beverly hillbillies / Stephen Cox. — 1st ed.
            p. cm.
    ISBN 0-06-097565-2 (pbk.)
    1. Beverly hillbillies (Television program).   I. Title.
PN1992.77.B46C6   1993
791.45'72—dc20   92-56266

93 94 95 96 97 ❖/RRD 10 9 8 7 6 5 4 3 2 1

This is dedicated to my loving parents, Gerald and Blanche Cox, who cared enough to give a wonderful home to three Irish children and one little Canadian.

And to our little Granny.

Also this book is for Paul and Reenie, two dedicated individuals who put so much love into the series.

Contents

Foreword by Buddy Ebsen ix

A Few Words from Roy Clark xiii

Thank Ya Kindly xv

Introduction xvii

✦ 1 ✦
Hills That Is: Swimmin' Pools, Movie Stars . . .
Hillbillies? 1

✦ 2 ✦
Cast Biographies 35

✦ 3 ✦
Conversations with Max Baer 103

✦ 4 ✦
"So They Loaded Up the Truck . . . " 120

→ 5 ←

Pity-full . . . Piiiiiity-full 144

→ 6 ←

Laughing All the Way to the Commerce Bank 150

→ 7 ←

". . . Movie Stars . . ." 169

Episode Guide 181

Afterword 239

About the Author 243

Contents

Foreword

"Tell me, Mr. Ebsen, when you all started making this 'Beverly Hillbillies' series, had you any idea it was going to be the smashing success that it turned out to be?"

That is the question most frequently asked by people everywhere about "The Beverly Hillbillies." Obviously, everyone who threw in with the show must have thought it had something.

It would have been fun if we had all written down our predictions and sealed them in a time capsule, but I don't think even the most optimistic would have slotted us for the number-one spot right from the starting gun. That includes Paul Henning, the charming little giant who dreamed it all up, for his talent is only exceeded by his modesty and conservatism. It was a funny idea, a good gamble, and we were all determined to give it our best, then see what happened.

And this is how I acquired the most diverting and enjoyable family I have ever known outside of my own.

Buddy Ebsen

Courtesy of Buddy Ebsen

Foreword

Postscript

Dear Steve,

September 26, 1992, marked the thirtieth anniversary of the debut of "The Beverly Hillbillies." How many of the current crop of prime-time television shows would you bet will be playing in the year 2022?

People ask me why "The Hillbillies" has lasted. The answer is obvious. The show is therapeutic. When I feel down, I watch an episode and then feel wonderful. Try it.

"The Beverly Hillbillies"! Long may they wave!

Buddy
Christmas 1992

A Few Words from Roy Clark

Recording star Roy Clark in a double role as Cousin Roy Halsey and Halsey's mother, Myrtle. *Courtesy of Roy Clark*

In 1968, I portrayed Cousin Roy in three episodes of "The Beverly Hillbillies." And in doing so, there were a few firsts that impressed me.

By this time, I was getting recognized in the business and had performed on most all of the variety shows, but this role was my television acting debut.

Also, Donna Douglas was my first screen kiss—not a bad way to start.

Finally, what really impressed me and what I admired most about the show was it was the first to use real country music as the theme. It almost amazed me because most country and rural shows used orchestras. The authentic theme, supplied by my friends Lester Flatt and Earl Scruggs, was great.

And because this field was new to me and I was nervous, all of the cast made me feel right at home and they were great to work with. Right from the initial read-through, I felt a lot better about it. I wasn't sure I could pull off the job of playing my own mother as well.

Buddy Ebsen invited me into his dressing room, which was like a little house on the set. He was studying guitar, so we picked a little bit. He invited me to have lunch with him and went out of his way to make me feel comfortable. You can see why I had fun.

A book on "The Beverly Hillbillies" is a great idea. The audience is out there, and the show was a part of people's lives for so long that it shouldn't be forgotten. Thanks to this book, it won't.

In fact, to this day, because of the reruns, people will walk up to me and say, "I saw you on TV last night!" and I thank them for watching. "Yeah, I sure loved that plaid suit ya had on."

I know immediately what that's from—"The Beverly Hillbillies."

ROY CLARK

Thank Ya Kindly

The author wishes to thank the following folk fer lendin' a heapin' helpin' of their time and effort to make this book look slicker 'an a greased hog:

Ken Allison, Carol Anderson, Rob Austin, Ken Beck, Carol Brady, Herb Browar, the late Gloria Buckles, George Carney, Ramona Christophel, Roy Clark, Kingsley Colton, the late Joe Depew, Peter Engler, George Faber at Viacom, Jeff Forrester, Tom Forrester, Dale Freeman, Mark Gilman, Jr., Phil Gordon, the late Shad Heller and his wife, Molly, Linda Kaye Henning, Bob Hope, John Horvath, Scott Hunker, Frank Inn, Jean Jensen, Nancy Kane, Sammy Keith, Cathy Keller, John Lofflin, Sandy Mailliard, Kevin Marhanka, the late Curt Massey and his wife, Edythe, Tim Neeley, Mark Noe (Park College Communication Arts Department), Louis Nye, the late Don Richardson (Silver Dollar City), Gabi Rona—photographer extraordinaire, Terry Wayne Sanders, Sal Scamardo at CBS/Fox, Al Simon, Dave Strauss, Ted Switzer, Jill Tandy, Fredrick Tucker, Elena Watson, Michelle Yohe.

Organizations: CBS/Fox Video; CBS Television; Columbia House Video Library (1–800–538–7766); Howard Frank Archives

(Personality Photos, Inc., P.O. Box 50, Midwood Station, Brooklyn, N.Y. 11230); Kellogg's Company; KMOV-TV St. Louis (CBS); Silver Dollar City; and Viacom International, Inc.

Most of all, a special tip o' the hat for the personal attention paid from my parents, Gerald and Blanche Cox, who taught me the pleasures of traveling. And to Paul and Ruth Henning, who opened this door and many others for me. (Ruth Henning's scrapbooks, which chronicle the extensive press coverage on the show, became an invaluable tool in constructing this book. Thank you for allowing me to study them.) And to the cast with whom I met, I only hope this book serves as an enjoyable scrapbook because I am certain it covers a very important part of your lives. Thank you to Max Baer, Donna Douglas, Buddy Ebsen, and Nancy Kulp.

To my original editor, Susan Buntrock, and to the editorial wonders at HarperCollins: Craig D. Nelson and Lauren Marino . . . Thanks for letting me "take the exam over."

Thank Ya Kindly

Introduction

If you can put a show on television that's something apart from everything else on television—then you're accomplishing something.

—*Jerry Seinfeld*

This book was first written during the latter part of my senior
year at Park College in Parkville, Missouri, in 1988. It was a
frenzied and anxious blur of time for me amidst exams, graduation preparations, emotional ties about to be broken—and this
book's deadline. This was my first book published, and for that
reason I am very proud of it. Also for that reason, I rewrote it.

I am happy to be able to augment the original book with new
stories, new, rare photographs, updated biographies, and, I hope,
an improved journalistic technique.

It's well known that there is not a show in television history
that has equaled the achievements set by "The Beverly Hillbillies." It's highly underrated, and it spills of genius, greatness,
and classicism: no other show reached the number-one spot in a
shorter amount of time. No other show can claim eight entries
in the Nielsen list of Top 50 highest-rated programs ever broadcast. One episode of "The Beverly Hillbillies" still holds the
record as the highest-rated half-hour program. Just think of it,
in 1962 there were many nights when half the television sets in
the United States were turned to "The Hillbillies."

This show can brag.

Yet it's doubtful that any other sitcom has received such despicable press and at the same time attained such fantastic ratings from the very beginning. The critics hated the Clampetts. The viewers loved Jed, Granny, Elly May, and Jethro, and for nine years the Hillbillies kept up their cornball antics while thriving in the Top 10 or 20. Ultimately, the word "hillbilly" took on a new meaning because of this television program. Financially speaking, this show, and other successful Paul Henning shows, played an integral part in keeping CBS afloat during the 1960s. As Buddy Ebsen said: "The Hillbillies got America's attention like a switch on a hound dog's hiney."

Truly, the creative minds for this show deserve recognition—something the Emmys never fulfilled.

I felt a book could serve as a forum of praise and celebration for the show, so more than five years ago I met with the cast individually, and I've since made some wonderful friends. The roots of these friendships stem from Paul Henning, the creator of this show and the one who trusted me with his "baby." I'm glad this book didn't let him down.

Before meeting with the cast of "The Beverly Hillbillies" I had my share of encounters with interesting—sometimes classic—personalities in the entertainment industry. There are times I can't forget: my conversation with Benny Hill about *Chitty Chitty Bang Bang*, a reassuring wink from Johnny Carson, lighting a cigar on the same match with George Burns, carrying lawn furniture around Eva Gabor's backyard with her, and my conversations with Mel Blanc, which I wish I had more of on tape, because I was never prepared when Barney Rubble or Foghorn Leghorn joined the conversation. It was fascinating to reminisce with comedienne Roseanne Arnold about the Hillbillies—her "favorite show of all time." And, maybe above all, my afternoon with Benji—perhaps the most unusual of them all.

Despite these experiences, meeting the cast for the first time was a thrilling trip into the surreal for me. I'm glad it didn't occur on one day, in one room—which might have been a bit much for this eager fan to grasp. It was ironic, but after all the fame and

Steering right into prestigious television history.

Courtesy of Paul Henning

fortune, the only cast member who actually lived in Beverly Hills was Max Baer, and he was trying to kick his identification with the character.

With the exception of a séance for Irene Ryan and Raymond Bailey who had died, respectively, in 1973 and 1980, I tried to arrange a time to speak with all of the regular cast in person. Because of my youth, I felt that no one took me seriously except Paul Henning, who didn't doubt the book's legitimacy.

It took a phone call from Paul to Buddy Ebsen to convince him to meet with this "kid" from St. Louis. When I went to Buddy's hideout, the Long Beach Yacht Club, I approached the tall, white-haired actor while he was joking with friends at the bar. I noticed he scanned the room a few times looking for me, but his eyes passed me up every time. When I finally introduced myself, Buddy looked down at me, a bit surprised, and said, "I'd buy you a drink, Steve, but are you old enough?"

I pointed to my Cutty at the table and headed toward it, hoping Jed Clampett—looking more like Barnaby Jones that day—was right in tow.

Even though Buddy was wonderful, I found some of his replies terse, and he explained that he was saving a lot for his autobiography. I can't thank him enough, however, for blessing this book with a Foreword. It was the stamp of approval from the show's star.

Since then, I've had the privilege of working closely with Buddy on his soon-to-be-published autobiography. I have cherished every meeting, every laugh, and every vittle we shared. It was during the process of editing his manuscript with him that I realized what a classic American original he is; I'm proud to say he taught me much.

In October of 1992, Buddy was en route to Branson, Missouri, to star in a one-man show at the Roy Clark Theater. He stopped in St. Louis for a few days and visited his childhood home, which was still standing, just across the Mississippi in nearby Belleville, Illinois.

It was the day after the tripresidential debate in St. Louis, and the press—every station in town—swarmed around Buddy as he showed his wife, Dorothy, around his old stomping grounds.

He saw, for the first time, his star embedded in concrete in University City, like in the Walk of Fame in Hollywood. And he even met St. Louisan Mickey Carroll, one of the original Munchkins from *The Wizard of Oz*, and they reminisced about the film they had both worked on.

But when I witnessed Buddy go into a full dance routine on the wood floor of the Blueberry Hill pub, it was like something out of the Ron Howard film *Cocoon*. This white-haired, eighty-four-year-old dancer, tall and lanky like Tommy Tune, was like a kid again; his graceful power was turned on. He bit his lip and with a sporty sort of "look at me" twinkle in his widened eyes, he danced the hell out of his tan cowboy boots. All of a sudden, he was twenty-two and smooth as ever. It was an eccentric dance in which he also used his arms, yet calculated and precise in movement. Everyone from the restaurant and pub was quietly amazed at his tap dancing. When he finished all that could be heard was clapping.

Strange but true, Buddy Ebsen was sought for the role Don Ameche eventually played (and received an Academy Award for) in *Cocoon*. Ron Howard must have recognized in Buddy the same transformation.

It was the summer of 1987. Nancy Kulp, who was in Atlanta, Georgia, performing at the Shakespeare Festival, eventually returned my phone calls and explained that she would soon be off to London, where she would sing and perform in a new sound-track recording of *Show Boat*. More letters and phone calls followed, but I just couldn't pin her down. She must have thought I was another crazy fan. Months later I finally met her at the Palm Springs getaway home of Paul and Ruth Henning. They had arranged a dinner for all of us, and Nancy had reluctantly consented to be interviewed afterward.

When she arrived, Paul and Ruth hugged her, then introduced me. It was Jane Hathaway standing rigidly in front of me! She leaned toward Ruth and said aloud: "You said he was young, but you didn't say he was *twelve*."

I tried not to slump, yet I enjoyed the jab from Miss Jane. It was like an insult from Don Rickles—sort of an honor.

That afternoon, we watched football, had dinner, then Nancy Kulp and I eventually retreated into the den for a private interview. She was an interviewer's delight: her mood was good, and she was outspoken, intelligent, eloquent, and very genuine. She spoke of the good and the bad very candidly.

After the book was out, Nancy told me she really liked it, and we kept up a nice phone correspondence. I'd make her laugh when I'd call and say, "Faversham!" instead of "Hello." ("Faversham!" is a line from the show; the Hillbillies mistook a butler's name for an amenity—like Aloha.) Contrary to her stiff appearance, she had a soft side. I remember one time when I called and she told me that one of her dogs had died. I can still hear her crying on the phone while I felt helpless.

Donna Douglas and I met at an Italian pizzeria she had chosen. She looked just like Elly May with her gorgeous hair that she still kept the same as her character's. No rope-tied jeans—

she was in a sporty powder-blue jogging suit that evening. Her old studio-bio said she was a vegetarian, but she ordered a combination supreme, so I knocked that question off the list.

Even though Donna was very polite and sweet, I never quite felt we were on the same wavelength. I was nervously picking up a piece of pizza when a saucy half-dollar-size slice of pepperoni dropped right onto my lap. I was mortified! At the end of the interview, we got up and I tried to make light of the red blotch on my pants. She showed her sense of humor and just laughed. At the end of the evening, Donna obliged when I asked her to whistle with her pinkies in her mouth as she had on the show.

Max Baer dodged me a bit. I finally caught up with him near midnight at the gates of his largest home. He looked great, but said he was too tired for the late interview he had set.

Max looked the same, too. He's a large man, muscular, tanned, with the short, dark hair he wore in the series, only now he sported a mustache as well. After a few more calls, and a few more weeks, Max gave me one of the book's best interviews. I think I just happened to catch him at the right time. Once during the interview, Max abruptly did a bit of Jethro: hypervoice, a bit loud, topped with a laugh. I almost didn't recover, I was laughing so hard.

It's been fun to keep in touch with Max. Conversations with him are never dull, and I always enjoy them. He's very frank, and, in fact, it's his mouth, he claims, that gets him in so much trouble. "I say whatever is on my mind, but that's me. Take it or leave it," he says. It's been interesting to quiz him about the show and its uniqueness in television. We've discussed everything from his famous father to whether he thought Nancy Kulp was a lesbian.

At the nucleus of this book is a short man, retired, alert, sharp, kind, and generous to a fault. I'm not sure why Paul Henning was so large-hearted, sharing with me his time, his talents, and his guidance, but I've never gone without thanking him—which probably embarrasses him. He's never been the type to toot his own horn, even though he's had one hell of a career to brag about. But that's okay, his work does the bragging for him.

At first, Paul seemed out of place in Hollywood. What was this hardworking gentleman doing in this business? Then I realized it was that conscientious, Midwestern work ethic. It was so nice to learn that the man who created "The Beverly Hillbillies" was a Missouri boy, too. He was born, raised, and started his career in a town very near Park College, outside Kansas City, where I was then finishing my degree. That was a wonderful icebreaker. Paul loved to refer to his roots and surprised me when he rattled off a list of cousins, brothers, sisters, and friends from back home that became the names of many characters who appeared on his shows.

I hoped that Paul, most of all, would approve of this book. When it was first published in 1988, he told me he was proud of it. Shortly after, Paul and I spent a few days together in his hometown of Independence, Missouri, and did some press interviews together to promote the book. He even visited my college dorm and other spots on the Park College campus. Then we had some time to tour his old stomping grounds.

All that was left of his childhood home were the concrete steps embedded in a small dirt mound at the front of the property. Paul took me to the Truman Presidential Library and Museum, and I'm sure God meant it as a wonderful gift that day Paul and I toured it together; he proudly reveled in stories about his long friendship with Harry Truman—also from Independence—and told me about the time he took his whole family to meet the elderly politician in his office.

At the end of the day, Paul and I sat in his sister's dining room signing copies of the book for each other. He inscribed a boxful for me to pass out to friends and relatives, and I did the same for him. I'm mighty proud of that.

So as things turned out, the year I graduated from college was the year my first book was published. Max liked the book. Buddy was completely surprised—and elated—and was gracious enough to do some press interviews with me to publicize it. I was amusingly aggravated though because he told better stories than he had when I interviewed him! Buddy eventually admitted to me that when we first met, he thought I was a fan just wanting to reminisce. Well, *I was.*

Donna Douglas didn't really like the book and even called me a "rascal." I suspect she would have preferred that I had not printed the story about Elvis Presley and her. Recently, Donna appeared as a guest on the "Sally Jessy Raphael" show dressed in the familiar rope-tied jeans and pink-checkered shirt, with her hair exactly like Elly's. (It wickedly reminded me of that "Baby Jane" syndrome, but I think Donna's got everything in check. She's just nostalgic.) Donna's face flushed when someone in the audience stood up and asked her about her alleged romance with the King. I think at that point she wished she hadn't met me. Donna also told me that she didn't like some of the photographs of her in the book. I quoted the longtime director of the show, Joe Depew: "It's impossible to photograph you badly, Donna."

In 1992, the remaining Hillbillies got together to celebrate the show's thirtieth anniversary. They had only seen each other a few times since the show ended: they were together at Irene Ryan's funeral in 1973 and a memorial service for Nancy Kulp in 1991.

At a 1992 American Cinema Awards tribute to Buddy Ebsen, I attended as Max Baer's guest. Donna was there. So were Paul Henning and Al Simon, the show's executive producer. It was great to see them all together, like family. Now, three decades after their show first aired, they were again posing for pictures together. It was a wonderful sight.

STEVE COX

The Beverly Hillbillies

1

Hills That Is: Swimmin' Pools, Movie Stars...Hillbillies?

It had never happened in the history of television, and it might never happen again. When the third episode of a peculiar little television show about a mountain family first aired, more than 36 million viewers cast votes electing the Clampett clan as TV's first family.

Although there were some winning reviews, television critics from coast to coast were appalled that the medium could stoop to such corncob humor. "We're liable to be Beverly Hillbillied to death," said TV conscience David Susskind. "Please write your Congressman." Critics detested "The Beverly Hillbillies," but America loved every bit of it, includin' their simple, down-home, corny gags. The show, which eggheads equated with mass stupidity, eventually cultivated a loyal following of more than 50 million viewers.

The Saturday Evening Post reported that "Hillbillies madness spread: juke boxes began blaring the show's banjo theme, army-and-navy stores reported a boom in plaid-shirt and blue jean sales, and network executives started ordering similar pastorales for future airing."

The decision was in: these Beverly-bumpkins not only hit Californy, they hit America—hard!

Courtesy of Viacom

This was not a mere rehash of filmdom's Ma and Pa Kettle, nor was it a takeoff on ABC's "The Real McCoys." For Paul Henning, the creator of "The Beverly Hillbillies"—and soon to be its writer, producer, and the driving energy force that fueled it for nine years on television—it was an idea that struck him while vacationing across the country with his mother-in-law. (Henning's wife, Ruth, hated long auto excursions.) He explained: "After five years of writing and producing 'The Bob Cummings Show,' in '59 I took this 15,000-mile motor trip to historical sites in the United States. Driving relaxes me.

"After leaving Lincoln's cabin in Kentucky, we drove along the two-lane highway facing the approaching cars at a closure rate of about 130 miles an hour. I wondered aloud what reaction Abraham Lincoln might have had if he were transplanted from the nineteenth century and suddenly found himself seated in the car with us.

"That idea kind of stayed with me. I wondered how, without being too magic, such a thing could be accomplished. I subsequently read a little bit about someone trying to build a road through a remote section of the Ozark mountains and the people actually would try to stop the building of the road. They didn't want to have access. Part of that, I'm sure, was that a lot of them made their living moonshining and they didn't want 'fereners,' as they called them, coming into the remote places.

"I avoided television for a while and wrote a couple of movies with Stanley Shapiro at Universal in 1960 and 1961. During those two years I used to get regular phone calls from Al Simon, urging me to create another TV series. He had been associated with me on 'The Bob Cummings Show.' Al was the president at Filmways. He really lured me away from writing movies over at Universal, and he convinced me to come up with a concept for television. He heard I liked hillbilly humor and offered to buy the TV rights for Ma and Pa Kettle, but I said no. 'If I'm gonna do a hillbilly program, I'm gonna do my own and create it myself.'"

Henning put his thoughts on paper and finally made the decision to do something. After that, things moved quickly. With the notion that comic strips are the most-read part of the newspaper, he created characters that were very much like those in cartoons—only they would be animated in live form. Days later, he had a luncheon appointment that would change his life. Henning was about to strike some oil himself.

Henning sat in his booth at the Brown Derby restaurant with Al Simon, Filmways Television president, and Marty Ransohoff, its board chairman. Henning explained his vision to them. He had his notebook with him and excitedly thumbed through the pages as he acted out the plot and described these fish out of water: "These hillbillies strike oil and move to a sophisticated urban center—which I first imagined to be New York City. But then I got to thinking of the cost of filming in New York, and it wouldn't have worked."

Simon and Ransohoff looked at each other with anticipation and allowed Henning to continue.

Henning explained the story, which he based on a few character sketches from his notebook, including an abundant list of show ideas that he had already jotted down. He also pointed out this was not to be mistaken with *Tobacco Road*, which he had seen and enjoyed onstage years earlier. "*Tobacco Road* is as funny as can be," he told them, "but you wouldn't want to see it every week. Poverty is depressing."

By the end of the lunch, the group had a handshake deal. Ransohoff immediately promised $100,000 of the company's money to produce the pilot. He was that sure of the show—and of its creator's talent.

The pilot film had funding, but the series had yet to be sold to the network, which also required a sponsor.

Simon and Ransohoff took the idea and ran. Simon was the genius of television, who had developed three-camera filming for a sitcom—long before Desi Arnaz took the credit. Simon explains why he agreed to this corn-fed comedy so readily: "To me, I thought automatically it was going to be the best thing that hit television in a long, long while. There was no question in my mind about it."

"First Thing Ya Know..."

After the script for the pilot episode, which was titled "The Hillbillies of Beverly Hills," was inked and passed between executives, the casting search was on. Casting was tedious for some roles, but Henning had specific actors in mind for others.

Jed Clampett, the cornerstone of the Clampett clan.

Photograph by Gabi Rona

"I always had Buddy Ebsen in mind," says Henning of the patriarchal Clampett role. "He's a big man, but he moves gracefully, as
a dancer would. He's kind of an ideal frontiersman, hillbilly, used
to getting around in the woods." Henning described his Jed as one
of simple, homespun honesty and dignity, the kind of Ozark
mountaineer he had known as a boy.

Henning approached Ebsen, who hadn't acted much since his
television role as George Russel, Davy Crockett's sidekick. Ebsen
was not much up for playing another backwoods role and later
said, "My agent had mentioned 'The Hillbillies,' and I wanted to
run the other way. I had played a lot of hillbillies, and I just didn't
want to get trapped again in that kind of getup with long hair and
whiskers."

But the script intrigued Ebsen, and being a practical man, he
knew he wanted to work. He took the part after talking with Hen-

ning, but first they had to agree on one aspect: "It sounded like everyone was going to be very funny—everybody except me," Ebsen says. "Which was fine, provided I was still the pivotal character. I told Paul that I gotta have control of the $25 million. If I do, I'll be the responsible member of the family and not merely the guy who's the butt of all the jokes! Paul agreed with me."

After being handed the role, Ebsen was patient with the screen tests of the candidates up for the rest of the roles. He remained, in costume, at the studio for many hours while hopefuls filed in to say their lines with him for the producers. This test on film was mandatory Simon explains: "There were many times in the room we thought somebody was very good and in the test they were not. We had to look at their on-camera presence. We had to see what the screen said."

Finding an actress for the part of Granny was the toughest. Henning and Simon frequented many Hillbilly bands and hoe-downs around the Los Angeles area and searched for the perfect geriatric they imagined. They thought they had found their Granny working at the Palomino Club in North Hollywood.

The makeup for Granny was tamed after the first few episodes. *Photograph by Gabi Rona*

The Beverly Hillbillies

"Finally, we found someone and thought, 'Gee, this woman's great. This is gonna work out,'" says Simon. "She sounded great talking to her. She said she'd have her nephew, with whom she stays, help her with the reading. When she came in and faced those cameras, she froze. She couldn't read! She was illiterate, but she disguised it cleverly."

Henning remembers that when he approached actress Bea Benaderet with the script, she said, "Oh, let me audition for Granny!" Henning pictured Granny as a wiry little woman, but let the well-endowed veteran character actress audition anyway.

"My actual statement was 'Bea, with those tits?'" Henning says. "Bea was stacked, you know. But when we did the test, she had seen Irene ready to go and do her thing. She pointed at Irene and said to me, 'There's your Granny!'"

Paul peered yonder to the other side of the studio where Irene Ryan, a petite lady weighing no more than a hundred pounds, was preparing to test. At the prodding of her agent, Kingsley Colton, she had visited Paul in his office earlier in the week to ask for the test.

Colton says: "Irene told me that Paul thought she was too young for the part. She said, 'My God, if they get anyone older, the actress won't survive the role.' Irene was, I think, sixty at that time." (Ryan was only six years older than Buddy Ebsen.)

Ryan tested with Buddy Ebsen, and Henning agreed with Bea Benaderet: this *was* Granny. The role of Cousin Pearl was given to Benaderet. In fact, Benaderet succeeded in stealing almost every scene she was in, so Henning knew this talented, versatile comedienne needed a vehicle of her own. Later he would cast her as Kate Bradley in "Petticoat Junction," another Henning hit.

Henning had already chosen the actress and actor for Elly May and Jethro before he met with Donna Douglas and Max Baer, Jr. "There was a girl who tested for Elly May, a redhead. She was a knockout. She was just sensational," Henning remembers. "We gave her the part, but she took another job at Universal Studios. I was so mad at her, I wouldn't have used her for free." Luck was with the shapely, blond ingenue Donna Douglas; the part was now available. Henning first saw Douglas in *Lover Come Back,* a successful Rock

Hudson–Doris Day film that he and Stanley Shapiro cowrote in 1960.

As Donna explains: "I was interviewed along with over a hundred other girls, I think. When they told me I got the part, I thought my heart was gonna burst right open. I was looking for a role like this, a family show. To me, it was an opportunity to do quality work. Something my parents and my son could be proud of.

"It was like God had trained me all my life to do that part. I already knew how to whistle and everything. And they never really had to give me any direction regarding Elly. I could tell you anything about Elly at any time, day or night. I knew Elly from day one."

In addition to the endless stream of women to choose from, there was the lineup of strapping young men for the role of Jethro. Saturdays were spent reviewing actors, among them Max Baer, Jr., but Henning had already decided on Roger Torrey. (Torrey later appeared on the program several times as navy frogman Mark Templeton, who courts Elly May.) Says Henning, "Off camera, Torrey *was* Jethro. I *knew* he was right. But on film, that big grin came on Max's face, and with that laugh—we had our Jethro." Henning opened his eyes to a comical side of the character that Baer had exposed in the test film.

Most of the pilot film was shot in five days on location at the Beverly Hills reservoir and on a soundstage at General Service Studios, Hollywood, in December 1961. Filmways built a cute little cabin-shack on location at Franklin Canyon in southern California. This was Jed's small mountain home. The patch of land they chose appeared as rustic and as rural as any place in the Missouri Ozarks. Meanwhile, Filmways was busy preparing the arrival of the Clampetts in the elite city of stars.

Henning, Al Simon, and Herb Browar, the pilot's associate producer, toured the back lot of MGM studios searching for a suitable mansion exterior; nothing pleased them. Finally, Henning scouted the Beverly Hills area alone in his Mercedes and came upon the perfect place: 750 Bel Air Road in Bel Air, California.

Photograph by Gabi Rona

The mansion-hideaway, owned by millionaire Arnold Kirkeby, a Chicago hotel magnate, was chosen as the Hillbillies' home. Kirkeby agreed to allow the studio to film the exterior of his home for the show—provided the grounds would be cleaned and restored to their original state after the crew had finished. (Kirkeby learned his lesson after Jerry Lewis and a messy crew had used the mansion as the location for the comedian's 1960 motion picture, *Cinderfella*.)

Kirkeby died suddenly in a plane crash just before the filming began, but the pending agreement was solidified by his widow. Filmways paid Mrs. Kirkeby $500 each day they filmed at the mansion front and around the massive courtyard grounds.

Aerial view of the Kirkeby mansion in Bel Air, better known as the Clampett mansion in Beverly Hills, around 1962. *Courtesy of Paul Henning*

The Kirkeby mansion in Bel Air (not Beverly Hills) was used as the exterior for the Hillbillies' home. In the early 1980s, it sold for more than $25 million. Couple a' mansions down the road a piece is the postpresidency retirement retreat for Ronald and Nancy Reagan. *Courtesy of Paul Henning*

The Beverly Hillbillies

"We persuaded his widow to let us film there as her husband agreed," remembers Henning. "We told her we would be careful and repair any damage that was done inadvertently. And we said we would not disclose the address of the mansion."

Eventually, the mansion became a recreation center for Max Baer, who became friendly with the Kirkebys' daughters, Carla and Carlotta, and regularly played tennis on the courts hidden to its side.

At General Service Studios, a huge set that re-created the Kirkeby mansion-front was constructed on Stage 4, the lot's largest soundstage. The elaborate interior sets decorated for the likes of Beverly Hills royalty proved costly. Built were an exterior of the house that led into the foyer, a parlor set that led into the kitchen set, the "cee-ment pond" swimming pool (modified from the studio tank), a Commerce Bank exterior, and an executive office for Mr. Drysdale. These sets and their lighting remained stationary so the crews could quickly dress, light, and shoot on the spot designated by the script each day.

Strategic Selling of the Series

The pilot was in the can, and now the job of getting the series sold to the network and finding a sponsor lay ahead. Originally, the show was offered to ABC-TV, which passed it by. Henning again had a strategy. He collaborated with Simon, and they decided to approach their favorite advertising executive in New York, Sam Northcross, who had worked with Henning on "The Bob Cummings Show."

Henning and Simon insisted on complete privacy regarding the pilot. They wanted this project to explode like a firecracker, so Northcross immediately flew out to Hollywood. "We picked him up at the airport and took him to the studio and ran the pilot for him late at night. No one was there," Henning says.

Northcross loved it and gave the account exclusively to the R. J. Reynolds Tobacco Company. Other sponsors joined in later. When Filmways approached CBS president James Aubrey with the idea,

Paul Henning among his Hillbillies. *Courtesy of Paul Henning*

he laughed aloud and bought the show instantly, but the vice president of programming, Mike Dann, openly "hated" the show.

"CBS took the show with one condition," says Al Simon, who became its executive producer. "The network had the right to premiere it on 'GE Theater' which was then hosted by Ronald Reagan. But the agency who sponsored the show turned it down, saying it wouldn't be right for their audience."

CBS had the pilot and wondered what to do with it. The network mucky-mucks, as the Hillbillies might have called 'em, still balked at the show's title. They preferred "Head for the Hills" or just "The Hillbillies." Network executives pushed hard for the title change, but Paul Henning wisely held out, and the choice he stood by was approved only weeks before the show's premiere.

The fact that the dubious program was rejected by GE's sponsor made a lot of top CBS brass think that it wouldn't succeed. And yet, wherever the pilot was previewed, audiences went wild with enthusiasm and laughter. Henning even brought a 16mm print to his mother in Independence and gathered around the kin for a private watchin'. After the final credits ran, Henning's mother looked at him and said, "And for *this* you get paid?"

Finally, CBS scheduled the program for the fall of 1962 opposite NBC's popular "Perry Como Show." During the summer before its premiere, Filmways and Henning felt CBS was doing very little to attract viewers, so they bypassed the network and began to develop their own strategy to promote the hill folks.

They quickly cranked out a series of special twenty-second personalized trailers — or brief previews — that would refer to the particular area. The Kansas City affiliate might want the "Heart of America" slogan to be incorporated, so the Hillbillies obliged. The

"Meet us in St. Louis!" The new cast gives a special Hillbillies' hello to the Gateway to the Midwest as they are introduced in this personalized trailer, shot especially for St. Louis's CBS affiliate, KMOX-TV. *Author's collection*

cast shot the trailers on their off hours and Filmways absorbed the cost, penciling the sum in the "advertising and publicity" column of their bookkeeper's accounts.

"The words 'Beverly Hillbillies' were not going to get a lot of people to watch the show," says Al Simon. "And the most important medium you could have was television. We began thinking the best thing to do was to get the Top 30 stations with the largest audiences in the United States that would be carrying the show.

"Paul wrote very funny trailers, and we had our publicity man contact every one of those stations and ask for their logos and told them we were doing personal trailers for that station. So before the show got on the air, everyone in those major markets knew about 'The Beverly Hillbillies.'"

By way of these previews, the characters of Jed, Granny, Elly May, and Jethro were introduced and viewers got a kernel of the corn that was about to captivate them. Their strategy worked: even before airing, the show had a built-in audience that had a hankerin' to see what these hillbilly folks was all about.

During the summer months of 1962, the show's publicity personnel were asked to adhere to a strict edict put forth by Henning:

Date: June 28, 1962
For the present, I would prefer that Buddy Ebsen, Irene Ryan, Donna Douglas, and Max Baer cease to exist as themselves. . . . The dissemination and publication of personal biographies, personal hobbies and idiosyncrasies, so-called "squibs," "blurbs," "plants" in columns and photographic layouts of them at home are to be discouraged by every means at our disposal! NO STORY IS BETTER THAN THE WRONG STORY! . . . and a wrong story is one that damages the television image of our hillbilly characters. . .

It was violently contrary to the whole indoctrination of the average P.R. man, but Henning was after quality more than quantity. Henning felt the audience would have trouble believing in the hillbilly characters if they saw publicity layouts of Max Baer boozing at a nightclub with some starlet or Buddy Ebsen steering his yacht.

Corn for corn, the Kellogg's Company was by far the best sponsor. *Courtesy of Kellogg's*

In fact, Max Baer was up for a guest spot on "Dobie Gillis," which would have aired in the half-hour time slot before "Hillbillies." Henning asked Baer to forsake the job: "In my opinion, if Max had appeared just ahead of us in a different role, his believability as Jethro on *our* show would have been largely destroyed," Henning says. For Paul, it was a fixation: only in-costume, in-character publicity was allowed for the time being—until the show got running smoothly and the characters were embedded in viewers' imaginations. Henning assured the cast that after a short period of sacrifice on their part, the success of "Hillbillies" would pay big dividends to them, since they would inevitably be in demand.

His ideas worked.

The premiere of "The Beverly Hillbillies" on that Wednesday night, September 26, 1962, captured nearly 50 percent of the viewing audience.

Two weeks later, *The Saturday Evening Post* wrote that "on location at the Bel Air mansion, the cast members got word of their

These Hillbillies can't believe their own ratings! *Viacom*

ascension to the top . . . Impulsively they formed a serpentine conga line and improvised a locomotive chant that went, 'We're number one! We're number one! We're number one!'"

Well, the Clampetts had arrived—in Beverly Hills, on television, and in America's heart.

It wasn't long until viewers knew every word of the theme song, "The Ballad of Jed Clampett," which told the story:

Come 'n listen to my story 'bout a man name Jed
Poor mountaineer, barely kept his fam'ly fed.
An' then one day, he was shootin' at some food,
An' up thru the ground came a bubblin' crude.
Oil that is! Black gold, Texas tea!

Well, the first thing you know, Jed's a millionaire.
Kin-folk said, "Jed, move away from there."
Said, Californy is th' place y' ought-a be,
So they loaded up the truck and they moved to Beverly.
Hills that is! Swimmin' pools, Movie stars!

Ol' Jed bought a mansion, Law-dy it was swank
Next door neighbor was pres'dent of the bank.
Lotsa folks objected, but the banker found no fault,

The Beverly Hillbillies

Musician extraordinaire, Curt Massey performed and recorded all of the background music for the show, then blended the tracks. Massey also wrote and sang the theme to "Petticoat Junction." *Courtesy of Edythe Massey*

'Cause ol' Jed's millions was a-layin' in the vault.
Cash, that is! Capital gains, Depletion money!

Well, now it's time to say goodbye to Jed and all his kin.
An' they would like t' thank you folks fer kindly droppin' in.
You're all invited back again to this locality,
T' have a heapin' helpin' of their hospitality.
Hillbilly that is! Set a spell. Take your shoes off!
Y'all come back now, hear!
    (Copyright © 1962 by Carolintone Music Company, Inc. Music and lyrics
                by Paul Henning.)

    The third verse of the theme was struck to bob the running time. The TV version was sung by Jerry Scoggins, who was a guitarist with a group called the Cass County Boys. In his career, he had recorded with Bing Crosby, the Andrews Sisters, and Gene Autry. Scoggins also recorded the Hillbillies' ballad on AVA Records to a limited release when the show took off.

Hello, Granny! Lester Flatt (right) and Earl Scruggs
performed the popular instrumental for the show's
theme song. *Viacom*

The banjo and guitar instrumental for the TV opening was provided by bluegrass legends Lester Flatt and Earl Scruggs. A year
after the show began, the sung version on Columbia Records sold
more than 200,000 copies and reached number forty-four on *Billboard*'s Hot 100 chart.

Production Notes

5:30 A.M.: Paul Henning routinely would arrive and set out coffee
and doughnuts for the cast and crew.

8:00 A.M.: Most of the cast would be ready to start work, or they
would be in makeup. If this was a read-through day, they were in
the office or on the set to recite their lines with the others. Present were the director, Henning, the cast, crew technicians, Frank
Inn or a substitute animal trainer, and the guest cast.

With one lonely 35mm camera, the shows were shot. Rarely
did they use two cameras. The shows were filmed in black and
white for the first three seasons, and the behind-the-scenes action

The Cee-ment pond: This monstrosity of a set stole a $20,000 chunk of the show's initial budget. It was only twenty-seven inches deep, complete with a filter and heating unit. Because a powerful air-conditioning system cooled the sound stage, the pool required nearly half a day to heat. Behind the Doric columns was a painted, half-round cyclorama of scenery that appeared to be Beverly Hills. Weeeelll, doggies, we was slickered! *Courtesy of Paul Henning*

was as hectic as it was on the General Service soundstage. In the offices, publicity men, including Ted Switzer and Lincoln Haynes among a variety of others, made their living promoting the show and honoring requests of affiliate stations. In Paul Henning's office, the pounding of keys on the manual Underwood typewriter could be heard down the hallway. Paul Henning would spend the day writing in his office, leaving only to solve a problem on the set.

Actually, this is the description of an average day, according to Phil Gordon, who played Jasper Depew in the early episodes. Gordon also became the dialogue coach and Henning's personal assistant during most of the show's run.

For Henning, the day started off dark. He arrived early—many times before the sleepy-eyed gateman. (Once, when Henning walked through the studio gates, he was denied entrance because the gateman didn't recognize him outside of his car.) Henning, as

At the time, this was one of the costliest sets constructed specifically for a TV series. More than $60,000 was spent to build a pseudomansion on a sound stage that would become the Hillbillies' residence. *Courtesy of Paul Henning*

a habit, put in long, hard hours and sometimes slept in his office. Mornings were a tranquil time for him to think, write, and concentrate on the scripts with no telephones ringing. Phil Gordon remembers those mornings: "You bet your ass, I had to get up early because Paul asked if I could meet him on the set at six every morning. Shit, I didn't know it got six twice! In the morning, on shooting days, we'd sit in a circle on the set before shooting and we ran lines. Then they'd go in their own dressing rooms and study by themselves and get ready with any makeup or costume that they needed to fix."

Irene Ryan required the most elaborate makeup job before donning the $500 gray wig and granny glasses that she perched at the end of her nose. Max Baer and Donna Douglas had a simple wardrobe of jeans, checkered shirts, and ropes for belts. Buddy Ebsen had only to affix a fake mustache, pop on his hat and coat, lace the boondockers, and he was on his way. Most days, he was unshaven, with frowzy hair and a comfortably rumpled image—

amply fitting for Jed. Ebsen could even enjoy a cigar while filming because Jed smoked stogies, too. Indeed, Buddy had it easy that way.

Not many knew it, but Raymond Bailey applied a convincing head of hair for his role as Drysdale. Every morning he slid the well-tailored salt-and-pepper toupee on his dome, fooling everyone who didn't know him well. When this hair was removed, he was rarely recognized walking down the street. This would upset him, says Nancy Kulp, who described him as a "publicity monger" who loved recognition.

One morning as the cast prepared for the day's shooting, a peculiar clumping was heard all around the soundstage. The director, Richard Whorf, called, "Cut! What the hell is that noise?"

There was dead silence.

Shooting resumed, only to be interrupted by the rhythmic clump-clump, clump-clump.

Finally, the mysterious noise was detected: Granny's boots were pounding the floor as she walked the set and Irene Ryan hadn't realized how loud it was. She agreed to try on a different pair of boots with softer soles.

"I tried another pair one day, but I couldn't seem to feel the character without those big army boots," Ryan told a *TV Guide* reporter. "They let me have them back when I promised to walk quietly."

That was a minor problem compared to the fourth-season complication: Filmways had promised Mrs. Kirkeby that the mansion's location would be kept secret. Just as the season was about to get under way, the address was discovered, leaked, and printed by *TV Guide*. Immediately, tourists and fans began driving by, knocking on the owner's door, and asking if Jed was home.

Henning describes the owner's reaction: "Seeing movie stars' homes is a big deal out on the West Coast. And although we had pleaded with every publication not to reveal the address, *TV Guide* broke the secret and all hell broke loose. Of course, this woman who owned the mansion was a multimillionaire. She didn't have to put up with that, and I couldn't blame her. She

Classic Misconceptions

- When the Clampetts arrive at their new Californy dwelling, they can't figure out what the strange chime (doorbell) is. "Every time we hear that sound, somebody comes knockin' at the front door," Granny says.
- Elly thinks the new bra that Miss Jane bought for her is a weapon, so she shows Jed. "Well, I'll be doggone!" he says, "a store-bought, lace-trimmed, double-barreled slingshot."
- Jethro thinks the refrigerator is a huge icebox cooled by "jus' one little tray a ice."
- Miss Jane informs Jed that she is covered by "sick benefits," and Jed thinks she's ill; Jane says all of Commerce Bank has "sick benefits," and Jed thinks the whole bank is down sick.
- A group of hippies perk up when they overhear Granny say she wants to go and smoke some crawdads. "But first I gotta get me a little pot," Granny says.
- When the Hillbillies meet Mrs. Drysdale, Jethro mistakes her fox stole for a real fox trying to attack her, and blows it to pieces with his shotgun.
- Jethro goes hunting and discovers a golf course, so Elly May decides to join in and play ball in her long, sequined "ball gown."
- Miss Jane tries to explain what a corporation is for, but the Hillbillies are baffled. Jed can't fathom why Mr. Drysdale doesn't want to hand money back to the government in taxes. Drysdale then tries to get out of it by saying that a corporation will "put more money in the hands of the people." The Clampetts drop pails full of cash out of the bank's penthouse windows.
- Jethro assumes a topless waitress is one who doesn't wear a hat.
- When the Clampetts take their first airplane trip, they reckon the flight attendant is really a kindly maid sharing her dinner with the passengers. The Clampetts are grateful and offer to help her wash the dishes.

called up and complained, and we had to give up location filming. The tragedy was that we were just about to go to color. This broke before we had a chance to film the exteriors in color. That was a real blow. We had to promise to stay away. She had just been beleaguered by tourists, and she had to get security people, shut her gates—it was a terrible mess. People actually would walk into her house and ask for Granny—thinking they really lived there. Can you imagine?"

The fourth year of filming not only did not include any more outdoor shots of the mansion, but never again did the series use any long shots of the courtyard and mansion-front. But by this

Classic Misconceptions (continued)

A conman tries to sell Jed the Hollywood Bowl. *Courtesy of Paul Henning*

• Jed neglects to answer a complaint served on him in a lawsuit because of its opening line: "The People of the State of California send greetings to J. D. Clampett." To Jed, it "doesn't sound much like a complaint." And as for answering it, he doesn't quite think he can send greetings back to "pret' near 18 million people."

• The Hillbillies think the billiard room in their home must be "the "fancy eatin' room" and the pool cues "pot passers."

• Jed thinks golf is something you shoot with a gun for sport—or you "club the varmits to death with these here golf clubs."

• Elly May attempts to cook Jed some "golf eggs" (golf balls). "I had to melt these rascals down," she says, "shell and all."

• When Jed becomes president of his own corporation, he's eager to get one of those "fancy leather lunchboxes" (a briefcase).

• When Mrs. Drysdale throws a garden party, Jed thinks it must be a gathering for all to pitch in and plant a garden.

---

time, the location was well established and the public hardly noticed.

CBS had finally converted all of its programming to color in 1965, and the first episode to broadcast that season showing the Hillbillies' true colors was "Admiral Jed Clampett."

Admiral Clampett had no problem with color, but Buddy Ebsen sure did.

"Stay out of the sun. No more tans or sunburns" was the order that Ebsen and the rest of the cast received from Harry Wolf, director of photography, as a consequence of the show's switch from black and white.

A birthday celebration for Paul Henning gathers casts and crews at General Service Studios. Note Raymond Bailey (behind left of Nancy Kulp) in glasses, minus toupee. *Courtesy of Paul Henning*

This stricture particularly affected Ebsen, who spent long hours in the sun during weekends, holidays, and vacations. He was, and still is, an avid sailor, with more than thirty racing trophies in his collection.

Ebsen had no intention of forsaking his seagoing ways, but for a while he had to squelch his activity and cultivate his pallor.

Wolf's order had to do with the complexities of the reproduction of colors by color film. If the actors' skin coloring changed from day to day, Wolf would be obliged to "make new film tests and adjustments daily in lighting and makeup, a procedure that would consume far too much time," a CBS press release noted.

As thorough as Henning, CBS, and Filmways tried to be, there were legal issues raised before and after the show aired. Henning recalls his visit with Gene Autry, who was associated with a musical group that called themselves "The Beverly Hillbillies." Henning sought a release for the name to be used as the title of the television series: "I remember going to see Gene Autry, and I'll never forget his answer. He said, 'I don't feel I got no holt on that title . . . go 'head an' use it.' I remember it because he kept saying *holt* instead of hold."

As with any success, there were the legal hassles. Directly after "Hillbillies" hit it big, a $2 million suit against Filmways was brought by four members of an early radio troupe calling themselves the Beverly Hillbillies. They eventually settled out of court for an undisclosed amount.

No sooner did producers of the show file that case in their folders when another suit appeared. This one, brought by writer Hamilton Morgan, charged plagiarism and asked a cool $15 million for the alleged theft of his "Country Cousins" television script that CBS had previously rejected. He claimed the similarity between "Country Cousins" and "The Beverly Hillbillies" was too great. The jury was hung, and the charges were eventually dismissed on "jurisdictional grounds" as the case was filed in New York and "Hillbillies" had been conceived of, shot in, and distributed from the West Coast. To eliminate further aggravation, a nuisance settlement was made.

These claims, among others, boiled Paul Henning. Through it all, Henning was an innocent victim tortured by those who wanted a piece of the successful show he had created. Henning says the lawsuits caused him not only high blood pressure, but invoked the most rage he had ever felt in his life. "Whenever you have something successful, there will be people who will try to stake a claim," he says. "Those lawsuits were like someone coming up to you on the street and grabbing your child, claiming, 'That's *my* child!'"

After the series ended, even a suit claiming ownership of the 1921 Hillbilly flatbed truck surfaced. Filmways battled and won the case, and eventually the heap was shipped down to southern Missouri for permanent display in a museum at the School of the Ozarks.

Without money coming in from the sponsors, the show would not have had the funds to pay its exorbitant legal fees, expenses, and salaries—large sums indeed. Originally, it was sponsored by the

As the Beverly Hillbillies say, "Eatin's gettin' easier, and much more fun!" And U.S. Government figures prove it. Today we have a higher standard of eating than at any time in American history. Our food is more than ever appetizing, convenient, nutritious, fresh, and abundant. And we enjoy this bounty for a smaller percentage of our incomes than anyone, anywhere, anytime in the world.

AMERICA THE BOUNTIFUL

Part of this bounty is the goodness of our land. The rest is progress. Until this generation of farmers, food processors, and grocers, working together, there was no fast, economical way to bring this wide world of eating pleasure to your table. But today at a typical food store you can select your menus from 8,000 or more items—thanks to the folks of the "vittles industries"!

FOOD IS A BARGAIN

A salute to the American Food Industry —farmers, processors, and grocers— from Kellogg's of Battle Creek.

Kellogg's OF BATTLE CREEK

R. J. Reynolds Tobacco Company and the Kellogg's Company. (The latter seemed especially appropriate to the critics: corn flakes for corny humor.) These two corporations were lucky to sign with a show that reaped so much mileage from successful ratings. Moreover, the cast was willing to go out of its way to film specialized commercials and ad campaigns for its sponsors. Jethro was constantly munching Kellogg's Corn Flakes on the show.

The funniest commercial was for Winston cigarettes ("Winston tastes good like a cigarette should"). One Winston spot directly followed a scene in the show in which Granny had just been introduced to a telephone. The commercial cut in after Granny had been smoking and talking to Cousin Pearl on the other end of the line, back home in the hills. Granny thinks Pearl, also puffing a Winston, can smell the cigarette smoke through the telephone line.

At that time, advertisers controlled more of the programming and wielded more power than the networks. R. J. Reynolds had a strong relationship with the "Hillbillies" cast, most of whom were smokers. One fan from Tennessee wrote to suggest that Granny smoke a corncob pipe, to which Paul Henning replied: "As to giving Granny a pipe—we sell cigarettes—although we once had her smoke a Winston by inserting it in the bole of her freshly made corncob."

R. J. Reynolds was a faithful sponsor but ended up pulling its support of the show in 1965 following the U.S. surgeon general's 1964 warning that cigarette smoking was hazardous to the user's health. (Congress followed up with tobacco-control legislation in 1969 that singled out television—unfairly, many say—and banned cigarette commercials from TV effective January 2, 1971.)

"Even before the ban, the surgeon general released a warning about the hazards of smoking," says Henning. "We got together as a cast and decided we better not do any more cast commercials for Winston as it would be bad publicity."

Sharing a warm moment on the set.
Courtesy of Personality Photos, Inc.

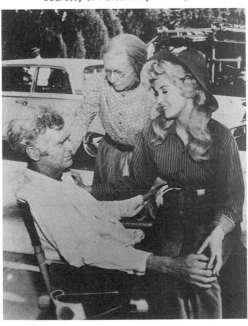

The show's shooting schedule was hectic. One, and, if necessary, two episodes per week were cranked out. They were usually shot in three days after a quick read-through of the script. From the reading Paul Henning would decide if any alterations were necessary, and production was guided by what scene didn't need rewriting. In an effort to accommodate the actors' schedules, as well as the crew's, Henning would retreat to his office and bang out another treatment of the script—sometimes handing pages to the cast just minutes before they were to be shot.

Each cast member had his or her working idiosyncracies. Buddy Ebsen had the ability to take "power naps" between scenes and used to sleep on the set in any old corner.

"He'd say, 'Come in my trailer and run some lines before we shoot,'" character actor Shad Heller said. "He'd fall asleep after I fed him a line."

Ebsen also had a Japanese cook come in every day to prepare meals in the dressing room's kitchenette. Ebsen lived it up, and he should have, as he was the show's "big name" and made the largest salary in the cast.

Max Baer, however, stayed to himself. Sometimes, if he saw that the cast was having a lot of fun, he'd join in. But usually he preferred to pursue his avid interest in the behind-the-scenes aspect of the filming, which years later resulted in several highly successful motion picture productions.

"One time Irene and I were on the set and Max came up to us excitedly," said Nancy Kulp. "He started explaining about this movie he'd seen the night before and he went into great detail about the shots, angles, and such. Irene and I kept nudging each other. He just rattled on. Finally, we got called for the scene. But a little later he came up and started on that bit again and talked us to death. He really has an eye for direction and how a picture should move. He's good at that."

Donna Douglas was the most cordial of the group. She was sensitive and sometimes emotionally fragile, but very easy to get along with. She required little to no direction. She *was* Elly. Donna spent hours autographing photos and personally responding to her fan

The Beverly Hillbillies

mail—she received more than any one else. Paul Henning recalls: "Donna asked me rather timidly if she could have some help in answering her mail, and I found she had about six thousand letters stashed in a box."

"She was very conscientious," says director Joe Depew. "It was impossible to photograph Donna from an angle that made her look bad."

After one series hiatus, the whole cast and crew noticed a complete change in Donna. She had become unusually quiet and passive and seemed to be going through a struggle in her personal life. The cast members tried to bring her out, but Donna remained withdrawn.

It seems that during her break in the filming, she costarred with Elvis Presley in the movie *Frankie and Johnny.* Some of the cast and working associates intimated that she fell in love and was completely consumed with the King of Rock 'n' Roll. "She didn't realize every girl he worked with fell in love with him, plus a million he didn't work with," says Paul Henning. "She really flipped out."

Some said Donna Douglas fell in love with Elvis after starring opposite the King in *Frankie and Johnny.* She returned to the "Hillbillies" set heartbroken.
Courtesy of Personality Photos, Inc.

Director Joe Depew remembers how this affected filming: "In the film [*Frankie and Johnny*], she shoots Johnny. When she came back to work, we had a sequence where she had to handle a pistol. She couldn't do it. She said to me finally, 'Look, I can't do this. I've asked Paul and he's gonna let me hold a rifle.' She wouldn't hold a gun, and I think [the Elvis incident] had something to do with it."

Douglas, when asked about this period, said: "I wouldn't interpret it as love or infatuation, but I was going through a rough time in my life then."

There were a lot of turbulent times on the set with Max Baer and Raymond Bailey. Bailey, the boiling, boisterous member of the cast, was brash and rude and would argue about anything. Buddy Ebsen says of him: "Ray was the sourest person I've ever met in my life." Ruth Henning remembers a promotional trip she made with Bailey, Nancy Kulp, and her husband. "We were going to a bank opening in Independence, Missouri, where Paul grew up. Ray got loaded on the plane, and when we arrived at Paul's sister's home, a big, historical, Victorian-style home, Ray made a loud remark that he thought it looked like a whorehouse. When

The progress of American astronaut Leroy Gordon Cooper was flashed over the screen during a prime-time episode of "The Hillbillies." This extraordinary debut mission for Cooper took him around the earth twenty-two times on NASA's thirty-four-hour Faith 7 orbit. *Courtesy of Paul Henning*

Paul's sister stepped out on the porch to greet us, Ray said, 'Are you the madam?'"

Joe Depew says, "You just couldn't take Ray seriously. He got mad at an ostrich one time. Ray got so damn mad because the ostrich wouldn't hit his mark that he threw a punch at it!"

Next to Bailey's, the second most energetic temper on the set was Max Baer's. "Maybe a tie," says Henning. Max was a hyper, loud sort who could impulsively say or do anything. There were some people around Max who were intimidated by his size and wired nature, but certainly not Buddy. And never Irene. Maybe that's why Max and Irene were so fond of one another. To Max, she really was a little grandmother.

As forceful as Max was, there was one time that Buddy Ebsen thanked God for it. This was a scene involving Jethro's attempt to convert the family jalopy into a helicopter by attaching a propeller above the truck, all connected to the engine. As the illusion of the car's rising was about to begin, the gag nearly cost the show its star.

Hillbilly Lingo . . . In One Easy Lesson

Corse youns would hear what the Clampetts was a-sayin' on all them there progrums ever' week. They talked in th' Hillbilly language o' the Ozarks. Here, in one easy lessun, youns can pick up a few o' them werds sose ya' know what we're yappin 'bout. This'l learn ya, so study up, now!

Frequent Phrases:

- "Set a spell."
- "Feelin' lower than a well digger's heel."
- "Ya tucked yer tail betwixt yer legs, didn't ya?"
- "I'll commence ta fixin' the vittles."
- "Fine as frog's hair."
- "Slippery as a hog on ice."
- "Err ya gonna spark [kiss] her, Jed?"
- "Ya got slickered an' ya shamed t'amit it."

Paul Henning prepared scripts with just such vernacular. Henning was a product of the radio age, where the word was what you were armed with, you better stick to it, and you bes' know how to use it. His hillbilly actors had to say their lines verbatim, without altering a syllable, unless Paul gave the word, so to speak.

Lingo t' Teach Them Goomers

Ainjun: Jethro cain't ever fix the truck's ainjun.

Argy: Elly don't argy with Jed, 'coze he's her paw.

Ast: Jethro ast Granny fer more vittles.

Banch: Jed has a banch in his workshop, yonder.

Bar: Did you find a cash bar [buyer] for th' farm?

Bobbed: Don't tear yore britches on that bobbed war (wire).

Bubs: The light bubs burned out.

Californy: A far west state where there ain't no snow.

Canny: Let Jethrine have a peeny's wuth of that rock canny.

Cheer: Granny sits in th' rockin' cheer sometimes.

Commence: Start or begin.

Daintz: Granny likes to square-daintz.

Dar: Destitute: They're in dar need.

Dawk: Granny's profession, a doctor (Doc).

Dreckly: Right away; "Fetch the truck dreckly, Jethro!"

Eench: Twelve eenches to a foot.

Et: Jethro et all his dinner—an' then some!

Fark: Knife, spoon, and fark.

Fer: For.

Ferener: foreigners. Fereners aren't welcome 'round moonshiners.

Flar: A rose is about the purdiest flar Granny done seen.

Ford: Granny says Jethro best come ford if he et the grits.

Gay-us: Put some gay-us in the tank, Jethro.

Goomers: Dummies or oddballs.

Grain: A color: Granny was grain with envy of Elverna Bradshaw.

Heerd: He ain't heerd a word ya said.

Hep: Elly cain't hep it, critters just a-foller her 'round.

Hern: It ain't hern, it's hisn.

Hillbilly: Somebody else.

Hit: If that don't beat all, don't hit?

Int: Int Elly's pet skunk a cute ol' thing?

Jist: Jist a dadgummed minute there, stranger.

Kag: A container: Kag o' beer, kag o' nails.

Lack: Jethrine was big—just lack her brother, Jethro.

Lar: Sure-fightin' word used fer someone not tellin' the truth: "That Drysdale's a damn lar."

Mess: A bunch: Granny'll fix a mess o' greens.

New-monie: A lung ailment, more serious than a varrus (virus).

The Beverly Hillbillies

Hillbilly Lingo (continued)

Nup: A hillbilly's "no."

Orl: The truck needs two quarts orl.

Pawpaw: A native fruit, kin to papaya.

Pie-annie: Cousin Pearl played the pie-annie at the local theater in Bug Tussle.

Polecat: A skunk.

Purdy: Elly May sure is purdy in a dress.

Raid: A bright color: She had raid hair.

Seed: He seed her first.

Sofy: What you an' yore girl spark on in the par-lor.

Spark: Kiss.

Thanks: Jethro thanks he's so smart.

Trappins: Clothes: "Jed's fancy Sunday trap-pins."

Turble: Granny thinks folks out here are turble.

Twixt: (Also betwixt): Between.

Varmits: What Granny calls Elly's critters.

Walled: Wild; Elly May is a walled deer.

Wil par: Jethro has no wil par when it comes t' vittles.

Worsh: Elly May bathes in a worshtub.

X: How some hillbillies still sign their names.

Yore: Your.

Younguns: Young ones: Elly May and Jethro.

Yurp: The continent overseas.

The camera was framed closely on Buddy and Max, who were sitting in the front seats of the truck. Two hydraulic jacks below the truck would raise it into the air, like an automobile in a repair shop. The jacks malfunctioned, and one side went up and the other side did not, so the truck began flipping over quickly.

Max describes it: "It was flipping the truck over on its side and it almost went all the way, but I jumped out. For some reason Buddy was on the driver's side. He saw what was happening and started to crawl out. The truck started to fall, and I held it back until other people could come and help me while Buddy scrambled off.

"If it had fallen, it would have landed on him and broken his back or neck," Baer continues. "Buddy didn't know what had happened until he saw it on film because they were still rolling at the time. I think I saw the dailies on it. Everybody was a little stunned by it."

Describing the cast succinctly, one writer said, "If Irene Ryan was the soul of the show, Nancy Kulp was its brains." Running with that, Buddy would be the class. Max was the wild energy, while Ray Bailey was the temper. Donna Douglas provided naiveté and behind it all was the heart, Paul Henning.

Photograph by Gabi Rona

The Beverly Hillbillies

→ 2 ←
Cast Biographies

Buddy Ebsen
"Jed Clampett"

Christian Ebsen, Jr.—that's his name, not a religious description—has gracefully entered his mid-eighties, and he and his third wife, Dorothy, steadfastly adhere to their motto "Use it or lose it." Over the years, the 6'3" actor has lost very little, except maybe a bit of his hearing.

Last year, Ebsen returned to the Midwest and performed his one-man show in Branson, Missouri, to wild acclaim. He was also returning to his first love in show business: song and dance. He's closely following George Burns in his career, he says.

The patriarchal Clampett doesn't have much to say about the nine years he spent playing TV's head-of-the-family hillbilly. He's written his own book now, *The Other Side of Oz.* The title refers to his originally being chosen to play the Scarecrow—and later being recast as the Tin Man—in the MGM classic *The Wizard of Oz.* He would have finished the role, but he became seriously ill three weeks into the filming when he ingested the powdery aluminum

Welllll doggies!
"Jed"
Buddy Ebsen

makeup used to paint his face silver. His lungs were coated and permanently damaged; it was so terrifying, he thought he might die. After his recuperation, MGM shoved him into a series of low-budget B westerns, "as punishment," he says. "I still have a tendency to bronchitis and a lingering cough because of that damned *Wizard of Oz*." (This was the first time I had ever heard anyone curse that movie.)

He veered off the journey to Oz, but he made the most of many roles, especially Jed Clampett. Ebsen still admires the ol' TV hillbilly, the millionaire who made *him* a millionaire. "Jed is a part of Americana now," Ebsen says.

Young hillbilly: Buddy Ebsen played a whiskery rube
many times before Jed Clampett came along.
Courtesy of Buddy Ebsen

The Beverly Hillbillies

Buddy Ebsen was born on April 2, 1908 in Belleville, Illinois, not far from St. Louis. He moved to Orlando, Florida, with his family when he was twelve.

Although his father owned a dancing school, young Ebsen spurned dancing lessons. He went to the University of Florida and Rollins College to study premed. Then he changed his mind about dancing. He went to New York almost broke and won his first Broadway role as a dancer in the 1928 Ziegfeld production of *Whoopee* with Eddie Cantor. His sister, Vilma, became his dancing partner, and for several years the team of Vilma and Buddy Ebsen drew strong attention in hot nightclub engagements, on road

Clint Eastwood, Buddy Ebsen, and Fess Parker (right) do a musical number with Danny Kaye on his CBS network variety show. *Courtesy of Buddy Ebsen*

tours, and in a string of musicals culminating with *Flying Colors*, a top revue of 1932.

Ebsen then felt the call of Hollywood, the glamour capital, where the lights shone brightly on the screen legends of the era. He was put under contract to MGM and danced his way through such films as *Broadway Melody of 1936*, *Born to Dance*, *Banjo on My Knee*, and *Captain January*, which teamed him in a memorable dance sequence with Shirley Temple. (Years later, in her autobiography, the former child star labeled Ebsen her "favorite dancing partner.")

He danced opposite Judy Garland in *Broadway Melody of 1938*, just before *Oz*, and went on to more films, theater, and nightclub work before he stepped into television, where he says most of the paychecks came from.

Ebsen, who in his career felt as many highs as lows, started off well in the medium of television. In his first successful television miniseries, he played George Russel, the rough-and-ready sidekick of Davy Crockett (Fess Parker) for Walt Disney. The Disney adventures became so popular with kids that the cartoon mogul spliced them together and released two feature-length motion pictures that did very well at the box office. *TV Guide* noted: "Davy Crockett stirred the country to the greatest commercial boom in frontier trinkets since the Indians sold Manhattan for a handful of baubles." Before then, nobody even *thought* about coonskin caps, and nobody was happier than Ebsen because the Crockett craze ushered him to further fame.

Along came more episodic television with "Playhouse 90," "The Andy Griffith Show," "The Twilight Zone," "Rawhide," "Cheyenne," and "Gunsmoke" among his credits. The first thing he knew, along came Jed, which creator Paul Henning had written expressly with Ebsen in mind.

Henning told *TV Guide* in 1969: "I was familiar with Buddy's work at Universal. I'd also seen him do a gem of a role as a hill man in *Breakfast at Tiffany's*. That, coupled with his work in Crockett, persuaded me to create 'The Beverly Hillbillies' with Buddy in mind for Jed.

The many roles of Buddy Ebsen. *Courtesy of Buddy Ebsen*

"I knew he had to be the fulcrum. He's a big man and I think audiences find it easier to identify with a big man; his dancing background made him graceful; and besides being a helluv an actor, he looked the part."

Buddy spent many days in jeans, a tan coat, and raggedy hat, with spirit gum dabbed on his upper lip to support his false mustache. On the set of "Hillbillies," when not practicing a tap-dance sequence or two, he usually retreated to an available chair or corner and fell asleep between takes.

"He's got that marvelous ability to sit down and catnap anywhere, anytime," said "Hillbillies" director Joe Depew. "That's what kept him going all those years. Bob Hope was that way, too. Sometimes it would be hard to walk over and say, 'Buddy, I hate to do this, baby, but we're on.'"

Buddy may have snoozed off screen, but on screen his performances rarely made viewers doze. After "Hillbillies," he found no

Paul Henning and the cast wish Buddy well as he goes to make the movie *Mail Order Bride* at MGM during the show's hiatus. *Courtesy of Paul Henning*

time to relax because he went almost directly into another series, portraying Barnaby Jones, a private investigator. The popular, milk-guzzling detective created by Quinn Martin provided Ebsen with several more years of steady employment in television.

Although his roles have been diverse, most fans associate him with Jed Clampett, which doesn't bother the actor at all. He says Jed's an "honorable, honest" person whom he was grateful to play. "There's nothing mysterious about the show's appeal," says its star. "It's the ancient theme of the Wise Fool. It's the country folk who make fools of the rich and sophisticated." And despite the harsh criticism the show received, he's always been proud of it. "Critics can be shit," he pronounces.

Former Filmways publicity man Ted Switzer recalls an incident that illustrates Ebsen's affection for Jed. Buddy was performing at the London Palladium when "Hillbillies" was the top show in England. "He did an act where he danced, sang a little," says Switzer. "And then he said, 'Maybe there's a character you folks

Max Baer and Donna Douglas congratulate Buddy Ebsen at an American Cinema
Awards tribute to the eighty-four-year-old actor and dancer in 1992.

Photograph by Steve Cox

know me from.' Then a beautiful showgirl brought out his Jed hat
on a plush, purple-velvet pillow.

"Buddy turned his back, put on the hat, and looked back out at
the audience and just said, 'Well, Doggies!' Then he set the hat
back on the pillow and resumed his show. The audience went
wild. They loved it."

Outside of acting, Buddy loves to paint, enjoys politics and lit-
erature, and is an avid student of U.S. history. He has studied the
life of Abraham Lincoln closely and wrote a play about the President called *The Champagne General*. Lincoln is a role he's long
aspired to play on film.

Irene Ryan

"Granny"

Irene was everyone's favorite.

—Paul Henning

If there ever was an actress who enjoyed a role, it was Irene Ryan, the wispy little woman who endearingly portrayed one of television's most memorable characters—Granny. She immortalized the word—in a video sense, you might say.

Having worked since childhood, Irene dabbled in just about every medium show business had to offer. She was trained in the "old school" of entertainment, learning early how to project to the back of the theater and belt out a tune so every note could be heard. She became a show-business institution in her struggle to the top and finally made it with her role as Daisy Moses, Granny.

She was born Irene Noblette in El Paso, Texas, on October 17, 1902, and at an early age moved to San Francisco with her parents, Sergeant James and Kathleen Noblette. She was an "army brat," she said, when she started her show-business career at eleven years old singing "Pretty Baby" at an amateur contest on the stage of San Francisco's old Valencia Theatre. Irene became a vaudeville headliner and toured across the country when still in her teens. From vaudeville, she stepped into radio, appearing with

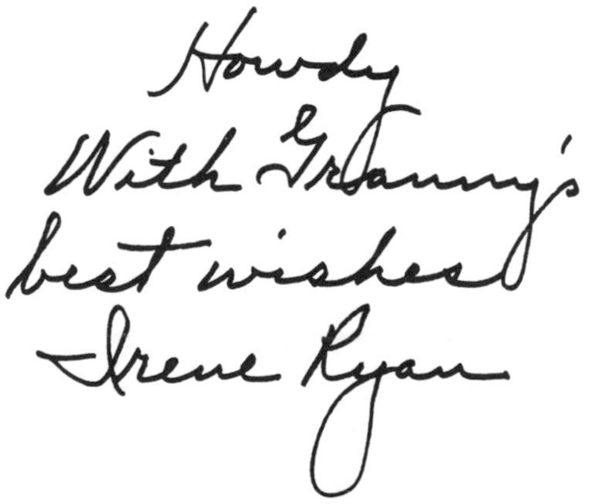

Howdy
With Granny's
best wishes
Irene Ryan

Photograph by Gabi Rona

Young Granny. *Author's collection*

Meredith Willson on "Carefree Carnival" in 1932. This led to appearances on "The Rudy Vallee Show," "The Jack Carson Show," and the popular "Bob Hope Show." At one point, she and her new husband, Tim Ryan, became a radio comedy team and starred in the popular "Tim and Irene Show."

Her radio success was a springboard to motion pictures that included *Desire in the Dust, Bonzo Goes to College,* and *Diary of a Chambermaid.* In between stints at movie studios Irene performed a nightclub act. Then, divorced from Tim, she worked as a single across clubs in America, honing a relationship with audiences that never died.

When Bob Hope toured military installations during World War II, several times he asked his pal Irene to join the troupe, and she quickly became known as "the gal who makes Bob Hope laugh." In their famous Christmas Caravan—Hope, Irene, Doris Day, and Les Brown's orchestra—they toured Germany, where they entertained U.S. airmen during the Berlin airlift before returning to the States to visit thirty-five leading cities.

Bob Hope: "The word 'delight' pops up when I think of Irene Ryan. She was a wonderful gal with a great sense of timing; she was a delight and always made me happy." *Courtesy of Bob Hope*

Reenie, as friends called her, worked hard in film and on stage, and when television lightened America's living rooms, she appeared in many shows, including "The Ray Bolger Show," "The Dennis Day Show," "Make Room for Daddy," "Matinee Theater," and "All-Star Revue." In 1961, she struck oil when she talked to Paul Henning about testing for the role of a granny in his new show.

Henning clearly remembers when he first discussed the role with Irene, a tiny lady who stood 5'2" and weighed just under one hundred pounds.

Henning remembers: "I said, 'Tell me, Irene, do you think you could play a hillbilly character?' She said, 'Oh yes . . . when I was in a stock company, we played a little theater in rural Arkansas. We were waiting for the curtain to go up, and we knew there were people outside waiting to get in and the manager wouldn't let them in. We asked, 'Why don't you let the people in?' He said, 'I can't let them in until you're ready to take up the curtain, 'else if I do, they'll sit there and whittle the seats away!'

"That stands out in my mind. It was hilarious . . . Irene qualifying as a person who *knew* hillbillies because of that."

After she got the role of Granny, she revered it, milked it, and molded the character; she popularized the age-old name into *more* than just a household word. "She could never eat dinner out," says her agent, Kingsley Colton. "She was mobbed if they recognized her. And when they didn't recognize her, it sometimes bothered her, though other times she was glad of it.

Unmasked: Irene Ryan often went unrecognized when she wasn't made up as Granny. *Photograph by Gabi Rona*

The Beverly Hillbillies

Photograph by Gabi Rona

"Nothing fazed her, that's why she was as great as she was. She was always kind to her fans—always! She was amazed at the overwhelming number of black fans who loved Granny; they approached her, swarmed her, and wanted to touch her. But it might have been children who loved her the most."

"One of my great joys as Granny is the way children take to me," she said in 1967. "Much of my fan mail comes from children. When I go on personal-appearance tours, children surround me. Sometimes they say that they wish their own grandmothers looked like me. Some of them just can't reconcile a 'modern-looking' grandmother with their *image* of what one should be!"

Reenie loved work, but had other interests. Besides enjoying her five o'clock Scotch, she loved to play bridge with her girl-friends, and after the success of "Hillbillies," she bought the largest black Cadillac she could find and drove it to work every day, sit-

Everyone asked Irene her age: "Let's just say I'm older than Shirley Temple, but younger than Sophie Tucker." *Courtesy of Kingsley Colton*

Ralph Edwards surprises Irene Ryan by honoring her on TV's "This Is Your Life." Ryan was at the Movieland Wax Museum to unveil the Hillbilly characters exhibit. Friends Meredith Willson, Arthur Lake, Buddy Ebsen, Paul Henning, and Donna Douglas were on hand to congratulate her. *Movieland Wax Museum*

The Beverly Hillbillies

Irene is escorted by her agent, Kingsley Colton, to
the motion picture premiere of *The Americanization
of Emily. Courtesy of Kingsley Colton*

ting atop a few pillows. "She also loved to bet a little on the horse races and had a season box at Santa Ana every year," says Colton.

During her run as Granny, Reenie saved her money and made wise investments. She went on tour during the show's hiatus with Max Baer and Donna Douglas, thus augmenting the nest egg she carefully guarded, and played Vegas, wrote a cookbook, and toured nightclubs in Australia. She treated her overwhelming fame with loving care, she treasured it, but she made sure she got the most from it.

After the show was canceled, Reenie took her fortune and established a scholarship fund in gratitude to her profession. She provided a trust fund of more than $1 million to award thirteen annual scholarships to outstanding theater arts students throughout the country in conjunction with the American College Theatre Festival. The Irene Ryan Scholarship program was inaugurated on April 23, 1972, at the John F. Kennedy Center for the Performing Arts in Washington, D.C., and today the program continues strongly under the guidance of the executor of her estate, Kingsley Colton.

Beneath the prim prairie outfits and steel-toed
boots, we never knew! This studio gag shot—one of
Irene's favorites—melded her head atop Betty
Grable's body. *Courtesy of Kingsley Colton*

After "Hillbillies" ended, Irene costarred in *Pippin*, an explosive
new Bob Fosse Broadway musical that also starred Ben Vereen.
Ryan was seventy and happy to be working (because she desperately wanted to continue after the "Hillbillies").

Her television costar Nancy Kulp remembers: "She called me
up and said, 'Hey, guess what they offered me? A Broadway
show!' I thought, 'Oh Lordie, what has she done?' I told her, 'You

"The Jug"

White Lightnin'. Mountain dew. Corn renderin's. Moonshine. White Mule. Mash. It all looked like pure, clear branch water, but Granny's potent private stock had set so long it was good for only two things: drinkin' and blastin' stumps.

Like many a mountain folk, Granny had a secret recipe for her illegally distilled whiskey. Nobody knew the exact ingredients, and after a few slugs, nobody cared. Two gallons was enough for a whole barn dance; two sips was enough for whatever ailed ya.

Of course, Granny claimed her nippin' was strictly for medicinal purposes. It was her "rheumatiz medicine." She admitted it wouldn't cure rheumatism . . . "but it'll make ya happy ya got it!"

Back in the hills, Jed first tried to lure Granny to Beverly Hills by assuring her she could run her still year 'round in California.

> GRANNY: *I run it year 'round here.*
>
> JED: *Yeah, but walkin' down to the still through the snow always makes you feel miserable.*
>
> GRANNY: *I might feel miserable walkin' down . . . but the way I feels comin' back makes up fer it!*

The Hillbillies set up the still for Granny's moonshine.
Courtesy of Personality Photos, Inc.

As the cliché says, much of life imitates art. And Irene Ryan mirrored Granny in many ways, includin' the jug. "She loved her Scotch," says Kingsley Colton. "With lunch she usually enjoyed a martini, but like clockwork, come five P.M., it was Scotch time." Max Baer said there were times when he'd tell her "she'd been drinking too many martinis and she'd better brush her goddamned teeth. And then she'd get into a scene and she'd hit me with a real pan instead of a phony one."

Granny hops over to "The Dean Martin Show" for a sketch poking fun at the Hillbillies. *Courtesy of Dean Martin*

have a new house, a cat with no name, a new Cadillac that you can hardly drive, why in the world?'"

Ryan had an "eighth-month-out" clause to escape from *Pippin* if she wished. But really, she lived for performing.

Irene received fantastic reviews from every single critic who saw the show. Her two musical numbers as the lusty grandmother Bertha were always capped by a steady, lingering ovation. She knocked every audience dead. The show became such a hit, with her two brief numbers as the highlights, that Motown records

The Beverly Hillbillies

released them, and at age seventy Irene had a hit single on her hands. All her reviews ran like these:

"Irene Ryan stops the show and receives a staggering ovation."
—*Ben Washer, The Hollywood Reporter*

"Of all the show-stopping in 'Pippin,' I think the ovation accorded Irene Ryan after she sang one of its best numbers, 'No Time at All,' was the most gratifying."
—*Richard Watts, New York Post*

A 1973 *New York Times* article written by *Pippin* choreographer Bob Fosse recalled how Irene relished her Broadway triumph so much that she stood in the wings and listened to the applause after she had brought the house down.

Fosse wrote: "Since the backstage is somewhat frantic—stagehands, actors, and pieces of scenery hurtling about crazily in cramped quarters, I suggested to her that it might be safer if after her exit, she continued on to her dressing room, eliminating the danger of being pushed or hit by scenery. You always had the feeling you should protect Irene . . . she was frail . . . she felt like a butterfly when you hugged her.

"Well, Irene looked me straight in the eye and said, 'Bobby, I've traveled 3,000 miles, given up a beautiful home in California, left all my dear friends—I really don't *have* to work . . . and all just to hear that sound. *Please* don't ask me to leave the wings until the last person has stopped.'"

Reenie suffered what the newspapers described as "a stroke" while performing in a *Pippin* Saturday matinee.

"We flew her back right away and put her in the hospital," says Kingsley Colton. "She came back from New York very thin and had not taken care of herself. They discovered a brain tumor, and she never came out of the hospital."

Colton later surmised that Reenie's mood changed suddenly in New York as a result of the tumor. "She said she hated New York and kept saying, 'God, I'll be happy when this is over.' Reenie never hated *any* cities. The word 'hate' was not in her vocabulary. She never hated anything. Then we suspected something was wrong."

Irene went into a coma and died a few weeks later, on April 26, 1973, at the age of seventy-one.

The following morning, the *Los Angeles Times* ran a large, bold headline above its masthead: IRENE RYAN, TV "GRANNY," DIES AT 71. The word "Granny," recognized as only one person, was all that was needed.

Services for Irene Ryan were held on May 1 in Santa Monica, California. Serving as her pallbearers were Max Baer, Kingsley Colton, Buddy Ebsen, Ralph Handley, Paul Henning, and Edward Sherman. Honorary pallbearers included Bob Hope, Bob Fosse, Al Simon, and Ben Vereen.

Paul Henning was asked to perform two uneasy tasks that day. Besides being a pallbearer, he delivered the eulogy, with a handkerchief in his fist. He cried at many moments, but went on to say, in part:

> *Today is May first. May Day. Mayday—the international distress signal. And that's exactly what the death of Irene Ryan brought about . . . a universal feeling of distress because she was known and loved all over the world.*
>
> *We mourn here in Santa Monica, California . . . but they also mourn in Tokyo, Japan, and Sydney, Australia. In Mexico City, in London, in Amsterdam, on the farms and ranches as well as on Broadway. . . . Irene was truly an international star.*
>
> *Yes, this is indeed a time to cry. Mayday! Help! We're in distress! But May Day has another meaning . . . a much older meaning. Long before it became a call for help, May Day was a time of joy and celebration. And I think that's the meaning Reenie would want us to have in our hearts today. Because if anyone ever had a full, rich joyous life, it was Irene Ryan. What could possibly be more fulfilling than to achieve success in your chosen profession? And not just success. A towering success! . . .*
>
> *"And the days of her years were three score and ten." Seventy wonderful years. Rich and fulfilling. And she enriched the lives of all who knew her, plus hundreds of millions who didn't.*

One of the last photographs taken of Irene Ryan, pictured here in costume for Bob Fosse's *Pippin*. *Courtesy of Kingsley Colton*

Reenie once told me that there was an old saying in vaudeville; I guess it applies to all of show business. "Always get off at the high point of your act. Leave 'em wanting more." Well, Irene, you certainly made your exit at a high point. God knows we wanted more.

Granny's Menu

Top 20 Vittles
Prepared fer the Folks

1) Catfish and apricot-gumbo soup
2) Possum shanks (Cousin Pearl's favorite)
3) Pickled hog jowls
4) Gizzards smothered in gristle
5) Smoked crawdads
6) Grits 'n' black strap molasses
7) Coot cobbler
8) Homemade pickled pawpaws
9) Sow belly 'n' hand-slung chitlins
10) Fatback and black-eyed peas (et on New Year's Eve to bring good luck!)
11) Possum-belly jam with a ham "omy-let"
12) Dandelion greens
13) Southern-fried muskrat
14) Hog jowls melba

Jed and Granny discuss the finer points of butter churnin'. *Viacom*

Granny finally trades the open fire for a conventional oven. *Courtesy of Kingsley Colton*

15) Deviled hawk eggs
16) Goat tripe
17) Boiled mule
18) Roast possum
19) Stewed squirrel
20) Ham hocks and turnip greens

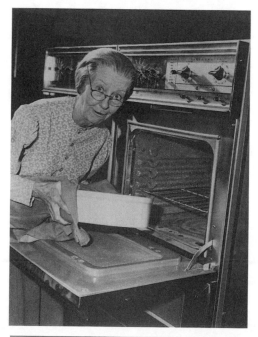

Granny shore did love her cabin-cookin' and so did Jethro! Every time she'd throw together a mess o' greens, Jethro would have 'em et before dinnertime!

Actually, the featured dishes here are real recipes that were mentioned on the show. At the height of the program's popularity, thousands of hill folk sent in recipes and suggestions for Granny to fix. Irene Ryan and writer Cathey Pinckney sorted all of the suggested recipes and put together *Granny's Hillbilly Cookbook,* published by Prentice-Hall in 1966. Irene Ryan was so proud of her book, she reportedly personally sent an autographed

The Beverly Hillbillies

copy to President Lyndon B. Johnson at the White House. Lunch!

Here is one of the recipes from the above list. Granny loved to share her culinary secrets. Besides, "How else is a gal gonna hold on t' her man?"

Deviled Hawk Eggs

Ozark Fixin's

a clod o' hard-cooked hawk eggs

a heap o' heated ham

a tin o' milky toads

a bit o' sweet spirits

a young onion

a quotom o' sweet pepper

a bit o' butter

a speck o' spicy salt

Ingredients

12 hard-boiled eggs

1 cup cooked ham, diced

1 can cream of mushroom soup

1/2 cup sherry wine

1 small onion, chopped

1 small green pepper, chopped

2 tbl. butter

1 tsp. seasoned salt

Fry up th' ham 'n' sweet pepper 'n' th' onion in th' butter 'til browned. Now dump in th' tin o' milky toads 'long with th' thick milk 'n' sweet spirits 'n' spicy salt. Keep yore heat mighty low 'n' stir so it's all well blended. Now toss in yore eggs and let 'em heat up easy like (5 minutes or so), makin' sure th' sauce never gits t' boilin'. Commence t' servin' in the fancy eatin' room.

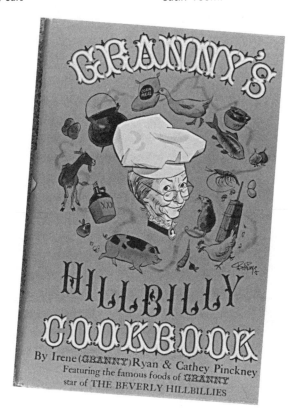

Photograph by Gabi Rona

The Beverly Hillbillies

Max Baer

"Jethro Bodine"

Max Baer, Jr., is a big guy. He weighs 210 pounds and stands 6'4". He's not one to tangle with. Like his father, world heavyweight boxing champion, Max Baer, who died in 1959, he has always had an avid interest in sports and acting, but boxing was not something they had in common. During the early part of his career, Max Jr. was disturbed when his father's shadow hung over his achievements. When "The Beverly Hillbillies" first began, Max kept the "Jr." in his name, but later decided to remove it as a sign of independence.

Max was born on December 4, 1937, in Oakland, California, and at the age of three moved with his parents to Sacramento, where he grew up and attended Christian Brothers High School. There, he channeled his energy into athletics, winning letters in golf, football, baseball, and basketball. He also won the Sacramento Junior Open Golf Championship two years in a row and later took the runner-up title in the men's tournament.

Baer's interest in show business began during his days in high school and continued at the University of Santa Clara, where he received his bachelor's degree in business administration with a minor in philosophy. He won letters in boxing and golf and performed in his first play, a student production of *The Male Animal*.

After graduation, Baer served in the air force for six months before going to Hollywood to find an outlet for his talents. He

Gratefully yours,

"Max Baer"

"Jethro"

Courtesy of Paul Henning

appeared in more than twenty television productions ("Maverick" and "77 Sunset Strip" among them) before landing his role as Jethro, a role he thought he wouldn't get. "Max was the only one who could have played Jethro," says creator Paul Henning. "Nobody could have done it better, I'm convinced. He was great."

Baer remembers he was not in good condition before he landed the role—physically or financially: "I was two months behind in my rent, and my weight had dropped from 210 to 188 pounds." That changed quickly when he signed the contract to star in "The Beverly Hillbillies."

A young Max Baer looks to the future: nine years on "The Beverly Hillbillies." *Photograph by Gabi Rona*

Late in the series, Max married, and he and his wife lived in Sherman Oaks. He divorced after the series ended and has remained single since.

Baer costarred in *The Long Ride Home* with Glenn Ford, George Hamilton, and Inger Stevens while still playing Jethro. When the final shows had been filmed, Max, who couldn't find work in Hollywood because he was too closely identified with Jethro, solved his problem by making his own movie.

"I wasn't important to anybody," Baer says. "They didn't need me for anything, and because I'm opinionated and stubborn as well as knowledgeable and reasonably talented, they didn't want to deal with me.

"So I put in my own money, $110,000 cash, my partner put in $127,000 dollars, and we made *Macon County Line*," he says. "That made us $10.5 million in rentals and $25 million at the box office. I produced and acted in it." Baer wrote the story for the film on the back of a "Beverly Hillbillies" script.

Baer followed with a mediocre film, *The Wild McCullochs* (starring Forrest Tucker), in 1975 and then *Return to Macon County*, starring Don Johnson and Nick Nolte, which did not do as well as the original. But he and his business partner repeated their box-office success in 1976 with *Ode to Billy Joe*.

After some calculating, Max realized he'd amassed a nice fortune with his films, and he invested it wisely. Currently, he owns homes in the Beverly Hills canyon, in Van Nuys, near Lake Tahoe, and in Las Vegas. With his successful business interests, he doesn't have to act anymore, but occasionally he steps in front of the camera for a cameo on television—"just to keep up my insurance card with the Guild."

His television appearances have been minimal, and that's the way he likes it. Among them: "Fantasy Island," "Matt Houston," which reunited him with his former costar Buddy Ebsen, and "Murder, She Wrote."

In 1991, newspapers reported that a Los Angeles jury awarded Baer $2 million after finding that ABC-TV wrongly interfered with his plan to purchase the movie rights to Madonna's hit "Like

Max Baer wrote, produced, and acted in the 1974 hit film *Macon County Line* after not finding any work for three years. *Courtesy of Max Baer*

The Beverly Hillbillies

a Virgin." Baer lost several rounds to ABC during the five-year suit, but finally won in the end, when a Superior Court jury voted nine to three in his favor. One lawyer representing ABC was quoted by the Associated Press as saying, "It's very difficult to defend a corporation against a likable actor." At the end of 1992, ABC was still appealing the verdict, and it has yet to produce a movie based on the hit song.

These days, Baer is a bit more accepting of the character he's known for and finds himself laughing aloud when he catches an episode of "Hillbillies" here and there.

"I like the show more now than when I did it," he says. "It's just a funny show. I can look at it more objectively, kind of like that's a different person on the screen, like those are four other people up there.

"I can appreciate Paul Henning more. I can appreciate the acting of the other people more. And I can appreciate what *I* did more."

Jethro in the Unemployment Line

Jethro never did find a job that satisfied his in-born curiosity. Heck, he done graduated the sixth grade; what more could a so-phisticated Hollywood playboy need? He once said: "I don't know why they call this the land a' opportunity. That's a laugh. Look at me. I'm edja-cated up t' here . . . and where does it git me?

"I can't be a dragoon . . . I can't be a double-naught spy. I can't be a brain surgeon. Too tall t' be a astronaut; too young to be President. What is there left?"

Here are the top ten careers Jethro aspired to:

1) Guru ("That name strikes a spark in my psyche.")
2) Hollywood agent/director/producer ("Starmaker C. B. DeBodine")
3) Protester/soul brother/flower child
4) Five-star general
5) Fry cook (Jethro's restaurant: The Happy Gizzard)
6) Atomic scientist
7) Psychiatrist
8) Bullfighter
9) Brain surgeon
10) Double-naught spy

Donna Douglas

"Elly May"

Sparkling Donna Douglas was born Doris Smith in Baywood, Louisiana, on September 26, 1933. Coincidentally, on the very same day, only years later, she premiered as a Hillbilly on television. That was an extremely happy birthday for Douglas, as the show catapulted her to recognition as one of the most beautiful girls in show business—or any business.

If Rex Harrison was Doctor Dolittle, then Donna Douglas was his Nurse. Douglas says she was born for the part of Elly May because of her built-in love for critters and the Elly May clothes she wore as a girl. "I was a real tomboy, but it was a matter of survival," she recalls. "I was the only girl on either side of my family, and I was surrounded by boys—an older brother and eight cousins, all boys." At an early age, she learned to jump off woodsheds, hunt, fish, and play football, basketball, baseball, and softball. "I was a pitcher on the boys' softball team for so long I was fourteen before I found out there *was* a girls' team."

Like the character she made famous, Douglas grew up loving nature, especially animals. *TV Guide* noted that "although she's not a true hillbilly, she is a native of the backwoods bayous of Louisiana, which, except for the elevation, amounts to the same thing." Douglas credits her understanding of Elly to the simplicity of her childhood in Louisiana: "I'd never trade anything for the summers we used to spend on my granddaddy's place. They let me

Lots of Happiness!
"Love,
Elly May"
Donna Douglas

Photograph by Gabi Rona

ride the horses, feed the pigs, and taught me how to milk the cows with both hands."

When Donna blossomed into her teens, the tomboy image soon wore off as she began cheerleading and winning beauty contests. In her last year at Redemptionist High School in 1949, she married Roland Bourgeois.

"I was seventeen goin' on twelve," she explained to writer Arno Johanson after she became a Hillbilly. "Frankly, we had no business gettin' married. All we had in common, really, was playin' baseball and basketball.

"We were much too young. But down home back then, no one seemed to frown on young marriage. That's what most girls think about. It's the thing to do, almost without thinkin', and that's what we did."

In 1954, Douglas had a son, Danny, and that same year she and her husband divorced. She was awarded the Miss Baton Rouge title and shortly thereafter became Miss New Orleans of 1957. These titles took her to New York, and Danny grew up with her folks outside Baton Rouge on a twenty-three-acre spread. Douglas's father was even an honest-to-goodness oil man who worked for Esso.

In New York, she really was like a hillbilly in a strange environment, but she held her own. She landed a job as the Letter Girl on TV's "Perry Como Show" and as the Billboard Girl on "The Steve Allen Show." (She was sort of the forerunner of Vanna White.)

Donna guested on such shows as "Thriller," "Checkmate," "Pete and Gladys," and "Mister Ed" before auditioning for the role of Elly May. In one memorable episode of "The Twilight Zone," Donna portrayed a woman who has undergone plastic surgery to repair her hideous face. She agonizes over whether the operation is a success, and when the bandages are finally removed, she's beautiful—but the doctors and nurses are pig-faced monsters in a world where they are the normal ones.

Just hours after Donna auditioned for Elly May, she had a car accident and landed in the hospital. She spent several weeks

＊アメリカで 最高の視聴率

じゃじゃ馬億万長者

ドナ・ダグラス
新緑の東京にお目見え！！

毎火曜夜 7:00〜7:30
4チャンネル 日本テレビ

Photograph by Gabi Roni

An advertisement for Donna Douglas's
arrival in Japan. *Courtesy of*
Ruth Henning

recuperating from whiplash, and "the only thing I could think of was getting out of there and starting work," she says.

"Right when 'Hillbillies' hit big, I was at home and my dad came home one night . . . everybody was so excited by the success of the show," Donna continues. "And my folks are kind of laid-back, quiet people. They are basic and don't make a fuss over everything. They don't know that much about Hollywood.

"My dad went out to the store and came back. When he came in he said, 'You know what? Somebody called me Jed Clampett.' It was so precious!"

Donna was proud of the show and made sure she did her bit to promote it. During its run, she traveled to Japan and Australia to greet fans and talk about Elly May. "That's the responsibility of success," she says. "The fans are the ones that put you there."

TV Guide: "Donna Douglas did more for blue jeans in 7 months, than cowboys did in 110 years." *Courtesy of Personality Photos, Inc.*

Donna Douglas participated in "Marineland Carnival," an hour-long CBS TV special in 1964. *Courtesy of Personality Photos, Inc.*

Donna Douglas was a phenomenon. The press loved her, and countless newspapers and periodicals put her face on the covers of every type of hometown TV listing around the country. She was a sex symbol, "a paragon of sweetness and virtue," writer David Marc put it. He went on to say: "Paul Henning tended to use [Elly May] primarily as an ornament, offering long D. W. Griffith–like portrait shots of her face and dressing her in tight flannel shirts and tighter jeans. For variety, he occasionally outfitted her in swimsuits and even formal evening wear."

Donna Douglas received most of the fan mail during the show's nine years, and today there are bold men in their late thirties who tell her she was part of their fantasy world as they pushed through puberty. More than one shock-jock on the radio has said this, and who knows how many individual fans have shared their thoughts?

During the seventies, the only thing the public heard about pretty Donna Douglas was that she was working in real estate in

"Merry Christmas from the critters and me!" *Photograph by Gabi Rona*

California. That was old news. "I began working in real estate in 1974 after the show ended, for about four or five years," she says. She was married a second time, to "Hillbillies" director Bob Leeds, for a few years after the show's nine-year reign, but they divorced around 1980.

Today, Donna travels, occasionally does a bit of country singing, and hopes to complete her second gospel album. On talk shows recently, she's held up a new Elly May doll that she markets and a couple of years ago she was also promoting a product called "Critter Cologne"—a $50-per-bottle perfume for cats and dogs.

She loves to work with young people and speaks frequently at church groups and Christian assemblies. Beneath her autograph she usually inscribes her favorite Bible passage, Proverbs 3:5–6: "Trust in the Lord with all thine heart; and lean not unto thine own understanding. In all thy ways acknowledge him, and he shall direct thy paths." "I care about young people," she says. "You can't just receive; you have to give back."

Donna still loves to be recognized as Elly May and makes appearances around the country—dressed in the familiar pink-checkered shirt and rope-tied blue jeans. She can still belt out a whistle through her teeth with a shrill blast that could peel the bark off a cottonwood tree at three hundred paces.

Donna Douglas toured the Sanyo plant in Gumma prefecture, outside of Tokyo. There she was honored by Sanyo officials, attended an autograph party, and appeared as the guest of honor at a reception given by *Hi Lady*, a Japanese woman's magazine.

Photograph by George Faber

Elly's Critter Countdown

It's been said that more than five hundred animals were used in "The Beverly Hillbillies." Everything from an ostrich to a skunk served as a pet for Elly May. Listed here are many of them there critters (or "varmits," as Granny called 'em) that Elly befriended. Included are the cuddly creatures and their names.

Bears: Johnny, Fairchild
Beetle: Cecil (Granny's weather beetle)
Bobcat: Bobbie
Buzzard: Daisy
Cats: Rusty (swimming cat), Matilda
Chickens: Eleanor, Henrietta, Rosie, Drusilla, Florence, Viola, Jane, Lillie, Martha
Chimpanzees: Skipper, Bessie, Maybelle
Crow: Freddy

Courtesy of Frank Inn

Deer: Maggie
Dogs: Arnie, Blue Chip (Mrs. Fenwick's unclipped poodle), Brutus, Hiram, Jo-Jo, Skippy, Wilbur, Ol' Duke (hound dog).
Duck: Gertrude
Eagle: Frieda
Fawn: Debbie
Goats: Clem, Thelma
Horses: Bessie (Pearl's), Silver-Trigger (Quirt Manley's), Ladybelle, Lightnin'
Kangaroo: Sidney
Kitten: Tommy
Jaguar: Jasper
Lions: Jethro, Herman (mountain lion)
Mule: Nelson
Ostrich: Miriam
Owl: Henry
Pig: Porky

Pigeon: Florabelle

Poodles: Claude
  (Mrs.Drysdale's),
  Collette

Possums: Wendell,
  Mickey (albino
  possum)

Puppies: Claude Fils,
  Claudette, Mimi,
  Jacques, Pierre

Racoons: Clyde, Davy
  Crockett, Elmer,
  Helen

Rooster: Earl

Seals: Whiskers, Ray-
  mond, Gloria

Skunks: Smelly,
  Charley

Squirrel: Mickey

Turkey: Herman

Donna Douglas says
there is no mystery to
her knack of working
well with animals.
The trick is to have
a genuine love for
them.

Courtesy of Personality Photos, Inc.

"Animals—particularly those that are basically wild ones, such as raccoons, foxes, and cougars—can sense the actor who dislikes them or is afraid of them, and they react the same way," she says. "Even when the actor tries to mask his real attitude, the animals seem to be able to see through his disguise and detect the truth.

"I'm like Elly May in that I'm genuinely fond of all animals. I think even the most skittish ones sense this and therefore will at least tolerate handling by me. I've found that some of the most unlikely animals actually enjoy being cuddled and stroked if it's done by someone they sense strongly to be a friend."

In one episode Elly May hugged a real bear. A stand-in stood by to film the scene, but Donna insisted on doing it herself. The bear was named Fairchild, and it had been raised from a cub by its owner and trainer, Frank Inn, who originally used it in the "Daniel Boone" television series. "That bear lived to be twenty-three years old," Inn says. "Donna wasn't afraid of it.

Elly's Critter Countdown (continued)

Donna was never afraid of any of the animals as long as I worked on that show. She knew I wouldn't endanger her, so she trusted me completely."

As a precaution, some of the animals—like the racoons and possums—had their teeth removed, nearly eliminating the element of danger. Inn retracts: "The only critter to make Donna jittery was an ocelot that was escorted to the studio by a trainer who was strange to the cast. The ocelot is a South American wildcat, you know, and it growled all the time. Donna wouldn't touch it until I came down to the set to oversee. It was harmless, but it did growl like it was gonna do something."

Chimpanzees, known to betray their keepers abruptly, never caused any problems—with Douglas, that is. She remembers a scene in which Skipper, the chimp, was supposed to leap from her arms into the arms of an actor and to nestle there lovingly.

"This actor was a very nice guy, but as we were preparing to shoot the scene, he grumbled that he wasn't looking forward to being 'pawed by that crazy monkey' and that the sooner it was over, the happier he'd be."

Skipper responded, says Douglas, as if he had heard and understood what the actor had said. Besides, it's doubtful that any red-blooded American chimp would willingly leave Elly May's arms to snuggle up with a mere actor.

"I practically had to throw Skip in order to transfer him to the man," Douglas says. Skipper refused to be held by him. Finally, director Joe Depew had to forsake the whole idea and get a rewrite of the scene.

The key to working with animals, besides the actor's knack, is the trainer. With Frank Inn, the Hillbillies had the best.

During the 1960s, Inn was kept mighty busy at General Service Studios catering to the needs of programs such as "The Bob Cummings Show," "The Adventures of Ozzie and Harriet," "The People's Choice," "Petticoat Junction," and "Green Acres" (remember Arnold, the pig?). Inn's famous mutt, Benji, has remained one of America's most celebrated pets since the 1960s. The original Benji was really named Higgins, but on TV's "Petticoat Junction" he was simply called Dog.

Inn pretty near turned the studio into a zoo while working with the Hillbillies. One reporter commented that the studio looked like Noah's Ark some days, when hordes of animals, it seemed, streamed on and off the premises. To serve all of the productions, Inn employed thirty protégé trainers, and his daily feed bill for the animals exceeded $400.

The first animal chosen to appear on "The Hillbillies" was Inn's own wrinkly hound dog, Stretch, who eventually became known as Ol' Duke. Inn fulfilled almost every request for an animal that Paul Henning put to him: kangaroo, ostrich, skunk, goat, possum. For many years, Inn remained Hollywood's top animal trainer and supplier of creatures for films and television.

"This is about the funniest thing I remember about working on the show," Inn says. "The show had Elly May riding a hippo as it's swimming in the cee-ment pond.

The Beverly Hillbillies

"That was the show that almost killed us all," said director Joe Depew about the messy ordeal with the hippo. *Viacom*

Animal trainer Frank Inn and Donna Douglas pose with a samplin' of critters: an owl, raccoon, and a possum package.
Courtesy of Frank Inn

"The pool is only two feet deep, and it took a full day to fill the pool with water. And after they got the water in, it took nearly another day to heat it well."

Inn explained how the four-year-old male hippopotomus, Herman, was "in love with" the female baby elephant, Lisa. The hippo would not go anywhere without his beloved jungle giant. Herman and Lisa's owner and trainer, Gene Holter, obtained the African hippo at age six months, and the Indian elephant at the same time. The animals grew up together in a heated stall. So, to get Herman into the pool, Lisa had to get in first and then step out—but stay within ten feet, dipping her trunk in the water so Herman knew she was close.

"We practiced this routine to get control," Inn explains. "Donna was in her dressing room at the time. We led the elephant and the hippo into the warm water, and as soon as they hit that water, they gave to the wants of nature real quick!"

"I mean they both let go, and that water immediately turned the most putrid green that you've ever seen. There was hippo shit swimmin' around that whole pool. Elephant balls and all. And the stuff that came out of the hippo hit its tail like a fan. It was a mess."

Inn removed the animals from the pool while some of the crew skimmed the water. When the job was completed, the water was still green. Inn suggested adding bluing to the water because precious shooting time was quickly vanishing. The chemical was poured in and mixed with boat oars.

"It was the most beautiful pastel color," Inn says. "It was thick—but beautiful, like an artificial ocean.

Cast Biographies

Elly's Critter Countdown (continued)

Donna on the back lot playing with Herman and Lisa. *Courtesy of Frank Inn*

"We got the hippo in the pool, and it was okay because it was empty by now. Then they asked Donna to come down, and first thing she remarked was, 'Oh my, what a pretty blue. Why is the water so blue?' I said, 'Well, Donna, the reason is the hippo is supposed to be swimming and in the clear water you could see the bottom of the pool.' She bought it!

"Next day at lunch, she gave me a heck of a whack across my shoulders. Somebody had told her."

Joe Depew remembers how the animals, while usually tame and under control, sometimes burst into rage. "We had a monkey that bit Irene one time," he says. "It bit her on the arm hard. He hurt her badly, and she screamed during the take, 'You son of a bitch!' We had to take her to the emergency room to make sure she was all right.

"Monkeys will be fine for years and years, and suddenly they'll turn on you," Depew adds. "They're messy, and I don't like them at all. Donna could handle them, though."

Of all her critters, Douglas says her favorite was Skipper the chimp, whom she used to swing between takes like a little child. "When Bessie, the second chimp, got big like Skipper we had to watch her," Douglas recalls, "because Max accidentally stepped on her foot and when she got big . . . boy, she had her eye on him."

The Beverly Hillbillies

Raymond Bailey

"Milburn Drysdale"

As a young man, Raymond Bailey aspired to be a banker or a stockbroker, but after he worked in these fields, he deserted high finance for a career as an actor. Ironically, many years later, he would become America's most famous banker and one of the all-time classic cheapskates. The road between Bailey's two banking jobs was a long one, which took him around the world several times and into various lines of work.

Bailey was born in San Francisco on May 6, 1905. Not much is known about his early childhood. He always preferred to speak of his life after high school, when he took off to Hollywood to become an actor.

He landed a job as a laborer at a movie studio when he arrived in Hollywood, still in the days of silent films. He hoped to be discovered by a director or producer, but instead he was fired for attempting to sneak into a mob scene. He then hitchhiked to New York to experience a stage career, but had no luck.

Young Bailey, "penniless and hungry," his CBS biography reports, "shipped out as a mess boy on a freighter bound for San Francisco." He spent the next few years at sea as a deckhand, seaman, and quartermaster, traveling to China, Japan, the Philippines, Hawaii, and the Mediterranean.

During the Depression, he became bored with the voyages and attempted to tackle Hollywood once again without success. He worked at a variety of odd places, including a pineapple plantation and a shipping firm, then decided to try out for community theater in Hawaii. Finally, his acting career began with a few roles in traveling stock companies. When Bailey returned to Hollywood in 1938, he launched his film career at Warner Brothers with, as he

Raymond Bailey

Photograph by Gabi Rona

put it, "several unspectacular parts in several unspectacular movies." His first role was in *Blackwell's Island* with John Garfield.

Bailey felt his more important movie credits included *Picnic, No Time for Sergeants*, and *Al Capone*. He also successfully tackled Broadway, satisfying his early ambition for stage performance. He appeared in *The Bat*, and off-Broadway productions of *Mister Roberts*, and *The Caine Mutiny Court-Martial*, among others.

In the newly emerging medium of television, he performed in over two hundred shows, among them "My Sister Eileen," "Dobie Gillis," "The Twilight Zone," "77 Sunset Strip," "Alfred Hitchcock Presents," and "Bonanza." He enjoyed the fame from his steady role on "The Beverly Hillbillies" as the unscrupulous Drysdale, and between seasons he acted in the theater. After "Hillbillies," Bailey could find no television work.

He and his wife, the former Gaby George of Sydney, Australia, lived in Laguna Niguel, California, until his death on April 15, 1980. His wife found him sprawled on their kitchen floor, dead of a heart attack. He was seventy-four.

According to most of the cast, Bailey was hard to work with. "He wasn't happy anywhere he was," says Paul Henning, who

Photograph by Gabi Rona

hired him. "He complained a lot, but he played the part perfectly." Bailey's temper would flare in an instant and calm in a flash. Many times on the set he would muddle his lines and get bitingly angry. Nancy Kulp, who probably worked the most with him, explained their relationship: "He called me 'Slim' all the time. He would blow up often, and I would go and calm him down and then he'd be okay. I seemed to be able to do that most of the time.

"I visited Bailey after the series was canceled at his home in Laguna Niguel. At first when he saw me, his eyes lit up. Then he said, 'Oh, it's you, Slim.' He liked me, but rarely showed it. And when I talked with him then, I remember we were out on the beach, and he was wondering why he wasn't getting any work. And nobody was coming to visit him. He talked for a half hour about negative things and griped about everything.

Nancy Kulp looked at this photo and said, "God, I had nice legs back then."

Courtesy of Nancy Kulp

The Beverly Hillbillies

It was rare to see Raymond Bailey act anything but grouchy around the set, said cast members. *Courtesy of Personality Photos, Inc.*

"God, he was aggravating, but I'd just say, 'Yes, Raymond, yes . . .' That was the way to handle him. When he'd blow up, people got so used to it, they just accepted it as normal. And that was Bailey."

Shortly after his death, *The National Enquirer* published a story about Bailey headlined: BEVERLY HILLBILLIES COSTAR DIES LONELY, SHUNNED BY BUDDY EBSEN. The article detailed how, after the series ended, Ebsen did not offer Bailey work in "Barnaby Jones" and said that this had made Bailey extremely bitter in his last years after his success as Milburn Drysdale.

"He alienated himself from everybody," says Don Richardson, a press agent who worked with Bailey. "Sometimes people hated to be around him, he complained so much."

Buddy Ebsen, however, found Bailey, "entertaining . . . he was always good for a laugh."

Nancy Kulp

"Miss Jane Hathaway"

Nancy Kulp was born in Harrisburg, Pennsylvania, on August 28, "A.D.," she adds. Actually, it was 1921. During her childhood, she attended seventeen schools in Pennsylvania and Florida, where her family eventually settled.

Kulp received her B.A. in journalism from Florida State University and studied for her master's degree in English and French at the University of Miami. She had aspirations for a career in newscasting. "Of course, television was in its infancy," she said. "And women had no place in television journalism at the time."

In 1951, Nancy left Florida and headed for the equally warm climate of Hollywood, where casting director Billy Gordon and director George Cukor thought she belonged in front of the camera instead of in the publicity business—her occupation at the time. She was given a featured role in *The Model and the Marriage Broker* only three weeks after her arrival in town. Her career was in first gear.

Her television shows during those early days of her career include "I Love Lucy," "The Red Skelton Show," "December Bride," "Playhouse 90," "The Jack Benny Show," "The Twilight Zone," "Perry Mason," "My Three Sons," and five appearances on "Matinee Theatre."

She had appeared in several motion pictures, including *Shane*, *Sabrina*, and *The Three Faces of Eve*, when the two longest series she acted in, "The Bob Cummings Show" and then "The Beverly Hillbillies," came along. Both had creator Paul Henning in common.

For four years, beginning in 1955, Kulp starred as Bob Cummings's bird-watcher friend, Pamela Livingston. In 1962 she won the role of Miss Jane Hathaway in "The Beverly Hillbillies," for

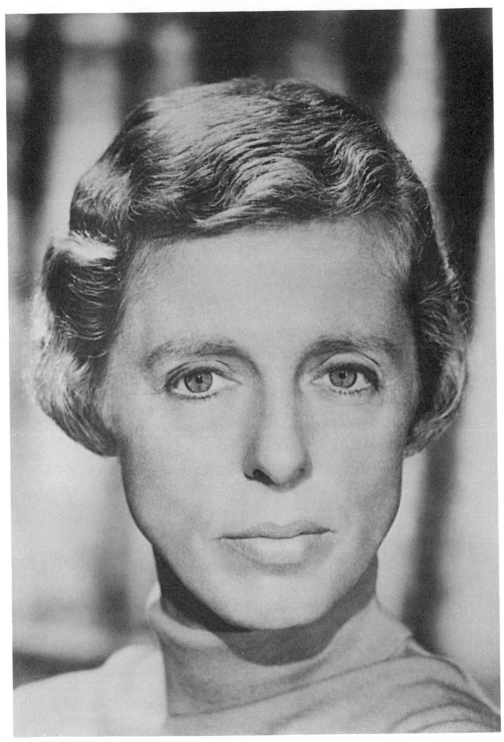

Photograph by Gabi Rona

"Pamela Livingston—as I live and breathe." Nancy
Kulp's regular role on "The Bob Cummings Show" led
to Miss Jane. *Courtesy of Personality Photos, Inc.*

which she received an Emmy Award nomination. Both shows
continue in syndication today.

Prior to and following "Hillbillies," she performed throughout
the country in dinner theaters and with repertory companies. She
even played the Wicked Witch of the West in a production of *The
Wizard of Oz* in Milwaukee. Later, she guested on such programs as
"The Brian Keith Show," "The Love Boat," "Simon & Simon,"
"Fantasy Island," and "Scarecrow and Mrs. King." She was also a
semiregular during the last season of "Sanford and Son." (Kulp
boasted: "Redd Foxx told me I was the only white woman he
could say he honestly loved.") And Broadway welcomed Nancy in
1982 in Paul Osborn's *Morning's at Seven*.

In 1984, Kulp finally surrendered to her longtime interest in
politics and unsuccessfully ran for Congress on the Democratic
ticket as a candidate for the House of Representatives in the
Ninth Congressional District in Pennsylvania. Her campaign led
to a well-publicized confrontation with Buddy Ebsen. Kulp, a

Avid football fanatic Nancy Kulp and her costar Ray
Bailey escort pro athletes Cookie Gilchrist and Earl
Faison and a friend around the back lot of General
Service Studios. *Courtesy of Filmways*

Democrat, and Ebsen, a Republican, had always squabbled about politics on the "Hillbillies" set. But it was Kulp's campaign and Ebsen's response that made their differences of opinion public.

Kulp said she had been sinking her "life savings and more" into winning the election. Ebsen recorded a detrimental, thirty-second radio spot that opposed Kulp. Her opponent broadcast the advertisement frequently, and Kulp felt she lost the race because of it.

For several years, the two actors who once worked together on TV's most popular show were at odds and did not speak to each other. Kulp was furious with Ebsen. She explains: "I just think it was unnecessary. I was infuriated with what he did. He was a great Jed, don't get me wrong. A great actor. But what right did he think he had?"

Buddy Ebsen and Nancy Kulp didn't *always* see eye to eye. *Viacom*

Ebsen counters: "You see, on national television, Nancy inferred that all the Hillbillies supported her. Well, I, of course, didn't. She was lining up endorsements from Ed Asner and other actors, and I didn't think that was fair. In fact, I wrote her and commended her on the campaign, but I said I didn't feel her opponent had national profile, so I made the tape."

Following this unhappy defeat, she became an Artist in Residence at Juniata College in Huntingdon, Pennsylvania. In 1987, she appeared as the Nurse in *Romeo and Juliet* for Georgia's Shakespeare Festival in Atlanta. Immediately after, she flew to London, where she took on the role Edna May Oliver originated in *Show Boat* (Cap'n Andy's wife, Parthy Ann Hawks) for a new soundtrack album. Nancy Kulp spent her last few years in Palm Springs, California, with several dogs that she dearly loved. She served on

Plain Jane: The quest for a man never
ceased. *Courtesy of Nancy Kulp*

Nancy Kulp in 1989.
Courtesy of Nancy Kulp

the board of directors for the Screen Actors Guild and enjoyed
cross-country trips in her automobile. She was married once ("on
and off for ten years," she once said) to Charles Dacus, whom she
credited for helping her cultivate an acting career. She divorced
him before "Hillbillies" and remained single thereafter.

Her last television interview was on "Entertainment Tonight,"
shot on her small farm in Connecticut. Kulp walked with the aid
of a cane, which she wielded like a prop. She appeared tired, slow,
and revealed that she knew she was dying of cancer. In the interview, Kulp seemed to be coming to grips with her condition. A
few weeks later, she traveled back to Los Angeles to receive special treatments. She died in Palm Springs on February 3, 1991.

Nancy, whose appearance hadn't changed much since "The
Beverly Hillbillies," was constantly questioned about her role. She
delighted in talking about the show and her close friend Irene
Ryan, or "Reenie," as she affectionately called her.

Months before Kulp's death, she and Buddy Ebsen ran into
each other, purely by coincidence, outside a restaurant. Both said
it was a relief after not speaking for so many years. Kulp described
it as a meaningful and forgiving conversation and felt quite con-
tent that their friendship had been restored—and was stronger
because of it all.

Harriet MacGibbon

"Mrs. Margaret Drysdale"

Harriet MacGibbon was a natural scene stealer, a skill she learned at an early age. She debuted on the professional stage at the age of eighteen on Broadway in *Beggar on Horseback*, starring Spring Byington.

This early performance paved the way for MacGibbon to gain more experience in the theater in such productions as *Anniversary Waltz*, *The Ladies of the Corridor*, and *The Front Page*, all before she

Photograph by Gabi Rona

The Beverly Hillbillies

Harriet E. Mac Gibbon

turned thirty. Her favorite role was Mary, the mother of Jesus, in
The Woman at the Tomb.

MacGibbon was born on October 5, 1905, in Chicago, Illinois,
the only child of a physician, Dr. Walter P. MacGibbon. She was a
great-grandchild of Dr. Elisha Deming, an Indiana physician who
was active in the Underground Railroad movement that helped
slaves flee to the North before and during the Civil War.

MacGibbon's family settled in New York, a natural locale for
her interest in theater to develop. She completed her education at
the Knox School in Cooperstown, New York, and her early ambition was to be an opera singer. She studied voice, piano, and harp
and planned to attend Vassar, but after appearing in a school play,
she changed her mind. Harriet was an actress.

Besides her Broadway performances, Harriet appeared in many
early television and radio dramas. She confined her professional
activities mostly to New York until the late 1950s. Her motion
picture debut was in 1961 in *Cry for Happy,* with Donald O'Connor, Joe Flynn, and Glenn Ford. Not long after, Bea Benaderet
suggested Harriet to Paul Henning as the right actress to play
Granny's thorn—Margaret Drysdale. Henning says he never
regretted his choice.

Harriet Elizabeth, as some of her friends and relatives called
her, was married twice. Her first marriage, to William Reno Kane,
ended in divorce; they had one son, William MacGibbon Kane.
Her second marriage was to Charles Corwin White, who died in
the mid-seventies.

Her son, William, became an art professor and taught at the
University of Rhode Island until his death in 1977; her family says
it was a crushing loss to Harriet. In order to stay busy after the end
of "The Hillbillies," she continued her love of cooking, taking
great pride in her cuisine.

Harriet MacGibbon, age 17, the year of her stage
debut. *Courtesy of Jean Jensen*

During her years on "The Hillbillies" as the brassy, tempera-
mental second wife to Milburn Drysdale, she guested on other TV
shows, such as "Dr. Kildare," "Hennesey," "My Three Sons," "The
Dick Van Dyke Show," "Bewitched," "The Smothers Brothers
Show," "Dragnet," and "The Ann Sothern Show." She also
appeared in the motion pictures *A Majority of One, The Four
Horsemen of the Apocalypse, The Absent-Minded Professor,* and *Son
of Flubber.*

Although her work was limited after "The Beverly Hillbillies,"
Harriet, a jovial, fun-loving type, enjoyed being remembered for
the series. She performed in commercials and did television
cameos, but basically retired in 1976 for health reasons.

"She gained an awful lot of weight in the last few years of her
life," Jean Jensen says of her cousin. "But she didn't care, she felt

that it was time to do what she wanted. It was really because of some spinal surgery she had and a battle with a cardiac problem.

"Her hair had turned completely white. It was gorgeous, and she kept herself very pretty. She got to where she could slap those false eyelashes on with both eyes closed."

Jensen remembers the lashes were once the point of a good "Harriet story": "We were at my house in Denver, and Harriet was visiting. A couple of us girls had a little too much to drink, and I remember Harriet fell asleep on the couch in this beautiful green velvet dress.

Mrs. Drysdale's precious Prince Claude of Burgundy. *Viacom*

"When I shook her to wake her up in the morning, she got up and said, 'Have you got bugs?' and she started swatting with the pillow at this little black thing on the couch—it was her false eye-lash!"

Harriet's own character could not have been more different from Margaret Drysdale's. According to relatives, she was a "solid individual and very generous and giving." On "The Beverly Hillbillies," she was closest to Irene Ryan, says her cousin.

In 1967, at Lenoir-Rhyne College in Hickory, North Carolina, Harriet told students, "Don't criticize until you can equal or do better than that which you're criticizing. Have your opinions, but keep your mouth shut." She also discussed her reason for drifting out of theater and into television. "Why did I go into television work? Money! Television work is safer, and there's more security, and it pays better than theater. I find it very interesting. It is not personally or professionally as rewarding as the theater. You don't have the actor-audience contact. TV is very impersonal, but TV work is fun and I'm happy to be a part of the industry."

On February 8, 1987, Harriet succumbed to a massive heart attack after a cardiac ailment that tugged at the last years of her life.

Bea Benaderet

"Cousin Pearl"

When "The Beverly Hillbillies" first aired, it started to become "The Bea Benaderet Show." Every scene that had Cousin Pearl in it was just about stolen by the actress.

Born in New York City on April 4, 1906, Bea Benaderet and her parents moved to San Francisco when she was five. She made her first radio appearance at twelve, singing in a children's production of *The Beggar's Opera*. Later, Orson Welles gave her a break and she began her career as a regular on radio's "Campbell Playhouse."

Early in her career, Benaderet played every radio show imaginable, from Gertrude Gearshift, Jack Benny's Brooklyn telephone operator, to Mrs. Carstairs on "Fibber McGee and Molly." She landed the radio role of Blanche Morton, George Burns and Gracie Allen's wacky neighbor, on their show. When the program

Pearl Bodine was Jed's first cousin.

Photograph by Gabi Rona

Bea Benaderet [signature]

went to television in 1950, Bea followed right along and proved as mighty an actress on the television screen as on radio. In fact, Benaderet was Lucille Ball's first choice to play Ethel Mertz on "I Love Lucy." Now, audiences who were emerging from the radio era into television could place the familiar voice with a face. Before and after "The Beverly Hillbillies," Benaderet appeared in guest roles on such TV shows as "Peter Loves Mary," "Dobie Gillis," and "The Danny Kaye Show." During the first four seasons

Bea Benaderet and the cast of "Petticoat Junction." *Courtesy of Paul Henning*

The Beverly Hillbillies

Cousin Pearl makes an entrance comin' down the newfangled fancy movin' stairs at the L.A. airport. *Courtesy of Filmways*

of ABC's "The Flintstones," Benaderet supplied the voice of Betty Rubble.

The role of Pearl on "Hillbillies" was given to her by Paul Henning, possibly her biggest fan. Henning had Bea in mind for Granny but handed her the role of Cousin Pearl instead. "She was a dedicated performer," he says. "She got herself a coach and studied hillbilly accents. She was wonderful!" A year after "Hillbillies" became the number-one show in the ratings, CBS asked Henning for another sitcom and he starred Benaderet as the mother of four girls in a little town he created known as Hooterville.

Benaderet was married twice and had two children, Jack and Maggie, from her first marriage. Her son, Jack Bannon, pursued an acting career and started out working at the studio as a dialogue coach, then acted in several Filmways sitcoms. Later, he costarred with Ed Asner on "Lou Grant."

Bea Benaderet loved acting and devoted almost her entire life to the profession. Her work was always praised by fans, although her talents as a comedienne, voice expert, and actress remain highly underrated by critics. For years she was known as the second banana, and when she finally became the star of "Petticoat Junction," the press rarely paid her the respect she deserved.

Shortly before her death, she was receiving radiation treatments for cancer and returning to the set of "Petticoat Junction" to act. After five episodes, she was forced to leave the show.

Benaderet was definitely a loving mother figure to the young actresses who became her television daughters on "Petticoat Junction." Says Linda Kaye Henning, who played daughter Betty Jo Bradley: "Bea's last show was actually just her voice. She was so ill that she remained at home, so it was written in the script that Kate was out of town when Betty Jo had her baby. In the show, she wrote a letter and regretted not being there when the baby was born and I had to sit and read the letter while her voice narrated. That was a hard show to do. Very emotional for me and the whole cast because we sort of knew she would not be returning."

When Bea Benaderet died on October 13, 1968, the business lost one of its most versatile performers. Her second husband, Gene Twombly, a sound-effects technician, died of an apparent heart attack just four days after Bea passed away.

About the Creator ... Paul Henning

Paul is a very fine writer. . . . The thing that I don't understand about Paul is why did he stop writing? He had three big hits. Here I am at ninety-six, I work every day. Paul, you ought to get a job!

—*George Burns*

As one writer put it: "Though William Shakespeare's name is probably better known in America than Paul Henning's, it is doubtful the same could be said of the two dramatists' work."

The seed for the hillbilly corn was planted long ago when Henning was a Missouri farm boy. It began in his Boy Scout days back

Paul Henning said in 1962: "My purpose in 'The Beverly Hillbillies' is to give the public pure escape entertainment . . . comedy . . . not phony 'heart' and synthetic 'warmth' dreamed up by a bunch of sophisticated writers sitting around in a smoke-filled room. I believe that the true 'warmth' and 'heart' can come only from the characters. I believe our characters have it." *Photograph by Gabi Rona*

in Independence, Missouri, where he spent summer weeks camping and hiking in the Ozark mountains. On his treks through the hills, he met and became fascinated with real hillbillies.

"I've wanted to write something about these lovable people ever since," Henning once told the press.

Henning was born on September 16, 1911, the youngest of eleven children. He worked his way through public schools by jerking sodas at a local drugstore. One of his customers, Harry Truman, advised Paul to go into politics. He might have taken the judge's advice if he hadn't gotten mixed up in the radio business to finance his studies at the Kansas City School of Law. Disillusioned with the legal system and unscrupulous attorneys, Henning decided to plunge into a career in radio, where he made his debut singing a Gene Austin impersonation on WDAF's "Night Hawk Frolic," a program, he recalls, that "unless you were drunk or couldn't carry a tune, you could be on." He took a job at KMBC Radio in Kansas City, and there he met the girl he was to marry, radio actress Ruth Barth. Their romance flowered because the station manager issued a ban on interdepartmental dating. As Paul Henning put it, "Like prohibition, anything forbidden was more fun." Meantime, he became the station's jack-of-all-trades,

George Burns (sans toupee) gets together with longtime friends Ruth and Paul Henning in 1988. *Photograph by Steve Cox*

The Beverly Hillbillies

Young KMBC radio personality Paul Henning escorts a radio contest winner to Hollywood, where they visit the Hal Roach Studios and pose with a few of the *Our Gang* personalities: George "Spanky" McFarland, Darla Hood, and Billie "Buckwheat" Thomas. *Courtesy of Paul Henning*

working as a disc jockey, singer, commercial scriptwriter, and sound-effects man.

Eventually, Paul learned that writing for radio paid better than singing on it, or at least that his writing was better than his warbling.

Ruth had already headed for Chicago to find work in radio when she wrote Paul to inform him of a job opening for a comedy writer. In 1937, Paul sent his unsolicited script for an episode of "Fibber McGee and Molly" to producer Don Quinn, and subsequently he was hired as a writer and moved to the Windy City. After a year in Chicago, he moved to California and immediately found work free-lancing for Joe E. Brown. Eventually, Henning became a staff writer on "The Rudy Vallee Show."

In 1939, he sent for Ruth and the two made plans to meet halfway and be married in Yuma, Arizona. In his letter, he gushed about their wedding and signed it, "Love, Your Good Yuma Man."

Paul Henning became a valued writer for "Burns and Allen" and spent the next ten years creating material for the couple's

Richard Whorf (back to camera) directs a brief greeting that was being filmed and presented to Paul Henning on his birthday. *Courtesy of Ruth Henning*

popular radio show, which made a successful transition into television. The Hennings and the Burnses traveled the country together and abroad, sharing a "wonderful relationship," Henning says.

Before Henning's break as a television auteur, he wrote some television scripts for "The Dennis Day Show" and "The Ray Bolger Show," and then he created, wrote, and produced "The Bob Cummings Show" for television in 1955; it was an Award-winning situation comedy about a Hollywood photographer with a roving eye for pretty girls. The show lasted five years, during which time Henning flirted with hillbilly themes in the scripts.

Changing course, Henning went to motion pictures and collaborated with Stanley Shapiro, who had won an Academy Award for *Pillow Talk*, on Universal's *Lover Come Back*. The Doris Day–Rock Hudson film was a huge success that earned Henning and Shapiro Academy Award nominations. The two also scripted *Bedtime Story*, starring Marlon Brando and David Niven. Brando later claimed the film was his funniest by far. (In 1988, *Bedtime Story* was remade—nearly verbatim—as *Dirty Rotten Scoundrels*, with Michael Caine and Steve Martin.)

The Beverly Hillbillies

Filmways urged Henning to return to television writing, so he reached back into his childhood for the inspiration for "The Beverly Hillbillies." By this time, it was evident that he was one of the first to master the situation-comedy genre.

In 1963, he wrote and created "Petticoat Junction," and he collaborated on "Green Acres" in 1965. For ten years Henning had a "trilogy," some said, of hits on network television. The name wielded power until CBS cut off all rural programming in 1971.

Paul's affection for the rural folk he wrote about led to the purchase of 1,500 wooded acres in Branson, Missouri. (Ruth Henning was petrified: "I thought Paul wanted to move out there and we had just built a house here.") The land became the Ruth and Paul Henning State Forest, which the Hennings donated—provided that it was preserved wild.

The Hennings have three children: Carol, Tony, and Linda Kaye. Linda, with whom Paul shares a birthday, costarred as Betty Jo Bradley on "Petticoat Junction" and was the only one of the children to pursue a career in entertainment.

It's a good thing Paul Henning didn't take Truman's advice to become a lawyer. Where would we have gotten such a masterpiece of unabashed rustic Americana? Andy Griffith might have stood alone.

Paul Henning's wife, Ruth, and son, Tony, were visiting the
soundstage when this shot with the show's star was snapped.
Courtesy of Paul Henning

Paul Henning stands tall in his success, with two of
his stars, Buddy Ebsen and Max Baer.
Courtesy of Paul Henning

Paul's associates' comments indicate the esteem in which Paul
is held. Al Simon says, "He is the best comedy writer around Hollywood or anywhere else. He accomplished things that no one else
I know of in the business could accomplish. He's one of my best
friends." Buddy Ebsen also calls him "one of my dearest friends. I
love him." According to P.R. man Ted Switzer, "He made the
show work. Truly a remarkable man." Bea Benaderet, quoted in
the *New York Times*, said, "The true talent of this show is never
seen." And Nancy Kulp said, "He's a genius in his field." *TV Guide*
prophesied that Henning would "go down in history as one of
America's best folklore comedy writers."

After the overwhelming successes he had with television, Henning retired and has lived in California's San Fernando Valley ever
since. The basic schedule he keeps today is nothing like the night-
marish routine he went through "minding the store," as he
describes his complete creative control. He told the press in 1962
that he felt the key to the success of a sitcom lay in creating a cast
of likable characters whom audiences want to see again and again.

And that is exactly what Paul Henning did. Again and again.

→ 3 ←

Conversations with Max Baer

Of all the cast members, Max Baer has probably dodged reporters the most. He likes his privacy, but consented to a rare interview when this book was first published. Since then, I've leisurely probed the topic of the show a bit more with him.

These days, Max seems much more nostalgic about his participation in the record-setting series. He recently pointed out that now he is the same age that Buddy Ebsen was when he played Jed. It gives Max a chill.

Here, Max shares some frank opinions about the series, his role as Jethro, and other factors relating to his break in the entertainment business.

How easy was the role of Jethro for you?

It came extremely easy to me. The lines weren't hard at all. It's one of those things. It's like some people can play basketball and some can play baseball. Some can hit. And others have to work hard at doing it. Everyone has an area that comes easier to them. I'm very poor in mathematics. Always have been. But philosophy and logic have been very easy for me. We're all different. My part-

Irene and Max always shared a close relationship. *Viacom*

ner is great in math and not especially good in some reasoning processes, although in math reasoning he is.

Max Baer is obviously different from Jethro, isn't he?

Oh, yes. That's because you're hired as an actor, not as a person. They don't hire you because you are what you play. They hire you for whatever reason you seem to be able to do whatever they want or their image of what they want. That's it.

What was the hardest part of the nine years on the show?

Trying to keep the level up all the time. It's like the best marriage in the world—you still have bad days. You're still gonna fight. Par-

The Hillbillies were TV's quintessential "fish out of water." *Courtesy of Paul Henning*

ents fight with their kids, and kids fight with their parents. Husbands and wives fight. Familiarity breeds contempt in many aspects. You spend as much time with a group of people as you do with your own family. Buddy, Irene, Donna, myself, and the cast spent more hours per week with each other than we did with anyone we were married to or whatever. You better be able to get along pretty well, otherwise it's going to be a battle because you don't want to go to work on a daily basis with people you don't like.

Did the cast get along?

Oh, yeah. But first of all it's like a dog and a cat. They may be enemies, but if you put a dog and a cat in a room together, they will learn to tolerate each other and get along because they know they have to do that to survive. I think that's the way most shows operate. It becomes very tedious for me to listen to all these people on the television shows tell how they're all a family and how they all love one another and are so happy together, when I know from experience that it's bullshit. They don't really get along. And they do have animosities. There are a lot of fights, but they aren't unusual. That's normal living. You may like or even love somebody, but from time to time, you're gonna get pissed off at them and tell them to get lost. I mean I yelled at Irene and she yelled at me, I'd get pissed at Donna and she would cry or something like that. Buddy would get angry with me and just turn his back on me, or I'd say, "Goddammit, Buddy, what's the matter?"

But that's natural. Not everything runs smooth. It's obvious to anyone with a brain in his head who has been fortunate to have a mother and a father that they fight and argue. Sometimes the closer you are the more you fight. But don't let anyone else pick on them, though. Don't let anyone else yell at Donna, Irene, or Buddy. I can yell at them. But if somebody outside of our little clique says something, I tell them off.

Max gleams at actress Judy Jordan, who plays chauffeur to Jethro—the big-time Hollywood agent. *Viacom*

The Beverly Hillbillies

Was the cast protective of each other like that?

Oh, absolutely. You get that way. At first you don't know each other, and it takes a while to get to know each other. There's certain things, then, that you don't like and certain things you do like. But you have to accept things you don't, just like a marriage. Just like your kid—you may not like a lot of things about your child, but you accept it. You can't just say okay, that's not my child.

What about your own family, you're not married now, are you?

No. I was married once. That was enough. I was divorced in 1971. No kids.

Somebody told me you knew Elvis Presley. Was he a fan of your show?

Yeah, I knew Elvis pretty well. We used to play touch football in Beverly Glen Park and then go up to his house in Bel Air on Perugia Way.

Photograph by Gabi Rona

There's some book that has a picture of me and Elvis and Frankie Avalon playing golf at Lakeside. He was a good guy. I met him in 1960. Donna had a very interesting experience with Elvis, which she doesn't talk about. Yeah, he was a fan of "The Hillbillies." In fact, when we were appearing at a rodeo in Memphis, he came backstage to see us and we talked for a while. I can't remember whether that was before or after the incident with Donna.

Did you think he would turn out like he did?

What, with the drugs and all? No. During the time I knew him, I never saw any of that involvement at all. But he always had a big entourage. Always.

Your nine years on "The Hillbillies" … were they lucrative for you?

They were lucrative for my ex-wife. She got everything. Actually, I didn't make that much. The first year of the series I made $500 a show. Second year of the series, I made $600 or $700 a show. Third year, we were the number-one show in the country, I think I made $800 a show. Most of the people who made the money were Filmways, the company who owned it, and Paul Henning, the writer, creator. Paul put in an awful lot of work on it, and I'm sure he deserved the majority of it. However, I believe even in that time, that as a cast, we were not paid very well. There were fringe benefits. We could go out and earn extra money. But we didn't earn enough for what we did.

How well did you do on the personal appearance tours?

We did reasonably well. We (Max, Irene, and Donna) would go out on the weekends and play state fairs and rodeos. Everybody on TV shows was doing them, Clint Eastwood, Dale Robertson. I'd make $5,000 in a weekend. We sure did a lot better than we did on the show.

"You'll be great in pictures, baby doll!" Starmaker Jethro tries his hand at directing voluptuous Gladys Flatt (Joi Lansing). *Viacom*

Didn't your agent eventually ask for more money?

Yeah, but, you see, I was kind of a maverick, and I knew that in business you need leverage. We all had different agents. Since Buddy was the star of the show going in, he got the most money. I think he got $2,000 a show the first year. That's all. Donna and I got $500 each, and Irene got $1,000. Ray Bailey might have got $1,000. I don't know what Nancy Kulp got. Maybe it was about the same as Donna and me.

So, I came up with an idea and said, "Hey, since Irene and Donna and I got along real well together and we went on the road together, we ought to get a mutual manager." So we got a manager named Eddie Sherman. He came up with the suggestion that he

CBS younguns: Gabi Rona snapped this photograph at a Beverly Hills Hotel pool party for the network's young stars. Look close and you'll find little Ronny Howard ("The Andy Griffith Show"), Larry Mathews ("The Dick Van Dyke Show"), Jay North ("Dennis the Menace"), and Rusty Hamer and Angela Cartwright ("The Danny Thomas Show"). *Photograph by Gabi Rona*

could go in and negotiate for the three of us together and make a better deal. The three together are leverage. I said, "Terrific."

What happened is that when he went in to try to get more money for us, which we deserved—and they were basically paying us damn near scale—well, Paul Henning got pissed off at Irene or Eddie Sherman, and somebody told Paul that Irene would walk off the show if she didn't get paid. That's what Eddie Sherman told the negotiators for Filmways. Paul really didn't like to get in the money end of it at all. He was basically the creative end of it. He was getting the lion's share, so I understand why he wasn't concerned.

Paul got a call from Filmways that Irene, Max, and Donna were gonna walk off the show. Paul Henning got crazy! He called up

Irene and said, "Hey, why are you doing this to me? You didn't have anything before . . . " And she didn't, which is true. He helped create a character that was terrifically advantageous to her. Irene got upset, and she got hurt.

But business is business. If they could've had us work for nothing, they would've, and we're trying to get the moon. So it's somewhere in between the two. Therefore, Irene relented and told Eddie to negotiate for her individually. That broke the link. Once they got Irene, they went to Donna, and the next thing you know they were all dealing with individuals again. We never got what we should have gotten at all.

And I was made out to be the heavy because I suggested we go with Eddie so he could package us together.

I have no regrets. Everything's fair in business. Somebody's gonna win, and somebody's gonna lose. We basically lost. C'est la vie. It's done.

On vacation from "The Hillbillies," Max Baer takes on a serious role in the movie *The Long Ride Home* in 1967. Baer won critical acclaim as a versatile actor.
Courtesy of Personality Photos, Inc.

Other than salary disputes, I heard you used to get pretty upset with yourself on the set sometimes when you delivered your lines wrong.

I try very hard to be good at what I am doing. Imperfection bothers me. It's not getting mad at anyone else, it's getting mad at myself. I get tremendously angry at myself in my inability sometimes to do what I thought I could do, at least well, if not better.

Another thing we used to say is the script is the "Bible according to Saint Paul." That was Paul Henning. The producer/writer is up in his room, and you can't have people on the set changing lines and action and everything. If you do, you slow down the production. In a movie you can, but in TV you don't have the time and luxury. So therefore, to have everything run reasonably smooth as a business, Paul Henning had to have everything done his way and all the words his way. So we were basically puppets. We'd do the lines exactly as they were there.

If there was a question, you'd get on the phone and call Paul and ask and he'd say yea or nay. Most of the time, he would agree. Also, he'd then be aware of what was goin' on. It was effective. However, it was also extremely frustrating because sometimes we'd get into situations where the people were trying to do their work—the script supervisor and director—by sticking to the dialogue. We'd all get tongue-twisting lines that we couldn't do.

That was a strict rule—not to change the lines—wasn't it?

Yes. But I was probably the biggest violator of that rule. I guess it came from my natural gut feelings. I thought, "If you wanted us to be puppets, you should have gotten dummies, stuffed them or made them out of cloth and wood, and had voice-overs."

Did you ad-lib a lot?

No, we didn't ad-lib at all. But I'd change some lines into the way I would say them as Jethro. After you do it for a while, you become the character and the writer starts writing for you. In the

The Beverly Hillbillies

beginning, you are doing what the writer has written. That happens on every successful television series. That's the way an excellent character is developed. Otherwise, you're never going to be able to grow any further than the original pilot screenplay. When you hire an actor, the actor's going to give you what you want plus some other things that you didn't even dream of.

Look, I went to college, and in college they teach you how to think. They don't teach you how to be a robot. When I went into the military, I wasn't very good at taking orders, and they want you to follow the leader. In essence, Paul was set up that way. It was follow the leader. One, two, three, kick. One, two, three, kick. It got very frustrating. It bothered Buddy, it bothered Irene, it bothered everybody. And I was always asking "Why is this?" and "Why is that?" That's just my nature.

Did you do this from the beginning?

Pretty much so. But they didn't want me for "The Beverly Hillbillies." They wanted somebody else. They wanted somebody who's since passed away, a real nice guy and good friend of mine, Roger Torrey. They tested him, four times. He was big, the right size. He looked like a country bumpkin, and I was tested later in the afternoon. I didn't think I'd have a chance anyway, so I just laughed at everything. I bumped into things and laughed when I made the test with Buddy. If I bumped into a doorjamb walking in, I'd say, "Excuse me!" and just laugh.

What did Paul Henning say when you wanted to change something?

He wasn't mad. Paul is a very bright man. And Paul is also up in a room, not down on the set. And sometimes things don't work. You can't write in a room and expect it to actually work because you may not have enough words to take you from point A to point B. They may be the wrong words for the action at the time. You don't have the time in television to be able to call the writer every five minutes when he's working on yet another script.

The show was Paul's baby, wasn't it?

All the way. Paul's a good guy, too. Look, I can criticize Paul and at the same time thank him. If it wasn't for him, I would've never had the job on probably the most successful television show of all time. At the same time, I can be critical because nobody's perfect and we all make mistakes, and I make more than my share and I'm more than willing to admit it.

Did the show seem to get sillier and sillier to do as the years passed?

Paul was running out of ideas. When you do 274 shows, that's a lot. How do you keep these people ignorant for such a long time? Later on, the jokes were a great deal more forced than in the beginning, when they were original. The first three years were the best.

Years later, when Paul approached you for The Return of the Beverly Hillbillies, did you feel it wasn't good?

No. I'm just too old to fully play Jethro. I'm a man, not a boy. Personally, I don't like digging up the dead bodies of old shows. I don't like to see the return of "Dobie Gillis" or "Gilligan's Island" and a lot of those.

Certain shows will lend themselves to growing up. We were almost like caricatures. We would not grow old gracefully because it would not be charming to have a forty-year-old man play this idiot. It's not charming at forty. It's charming at eighteen.

To have Buddy come back, that's fine. If Irene was alive, to have her do it, that's fine. Agewise, they didn't change. We did. If they would have two new people instead of Donna and myself, maybe they would have something, and that was actually my suggestion. The premise bothered me. And I don't want to play Jethro for the rest of my life.

If the script had been much better, would you have done it?

No. As a matter of fact, for the last twenty years I've only done about ten parts as an actor. Reason being, that's what I wanted to do. I didn't want to do Jethro. I rarely do guests on a weekly series, but I have done about one a year lately, just to keep up my insurance with the Screen Actors Guild. I just don't have to. I made a lot of money in movies with the ones that I own. So I don't have to work. I'm not going to do something I don't want to do.

Did you watch the movie when it aired?

No. I heard it was poor. It didn't have the charm. Granny wasn't there, and to me, Granny was the show. Buddy was a great straight man, a terrific actor, and a nice guy, but Irene was it. Without Abbott there wouldn't be any Costello. Without Costello, there wouldn't be anything. The comic makes it work. Irene was the

Jethro's a five-star general tugged at by beauties (Devon Blaine, Mady Maguire).
Courtesy of Personality Photos, Inc.

foil. Irene and myself got the most, or were the brunt of the most jokes, not Buddy.

How did Irene feel about the success?

Irene was just happy to be working. She busted her hump for a lot of years and never really made it in this business, and when she got her shot, she was gonna ride that home into the sunset. She never wanted to make any waves.

That's why she didn't buck Paul Henning when the negotiations came down to money. She figured she'd have enough money to live on the rest of her life, which she did. She would rather not lose the job. She was so afraid of that, and that was one thing that really bothered me and I could see it. It was my first real understanding of somebody that was older. She'd been in the business forty years, had a chance to really do something, and the network and Filmways used leverage against her and scared her. She thought she'd never get another chance like this, so she wasn't gonna risk losing it. I saw the fear in her. I was so young, I didn't give a shit. I was naive.

Did you like the job itself?

Let's put it this way, I really liked the first couple of years with Richard Whorf directing. After that, it became very mechanical. Whorf had Joe Depew as an assistant director; Joe was a real nice guy. He was brought in after Whorf was fired to do exactly what Paul Henning wanted—make sure the lines were said, do the shots. Joe had never directed before. He was basically a sergeant at arms. I liked him. But Richard Whorf was an actor first. He was in *Yankee Doodle Dandy* as Cagney's partner.

I liked the job, but there were confrontations. If I changed every line that [Paul Henning] wrote, he'd feel he had no worth. If I'd do every line that he wrote, I'd feel I had no worth. Now somewhere in between, there's a happy medium. And that was the constant battle. Buddy fought the battle. Irene did. Most of them would gripe and bitch, then let it go and do it. I was more reluctant. I'd go to the phone and call him and call him and call him. I'd call him more than anyone else and it became irritating to everybody, but that was the price they had to pay with me.

I knew I was dispensable. Nobody was indispensable on the show. Maybe Irene. But I had to do it. Sometimes the frustration would build up and I'd get pissed off and I'd break something, but it was due to my own frustration.

I could have walked off and never done it again. I always had that choice.

Did you mind playing Jethrine?

In one regard. I would go in and play Jethro in the morning. I'd take all the makeup off and put on a base which got rid of the beard that showed up in black and white. Play Jethrine. Then take the makeup off and play Jethro again. I'd do that two and three

"Ain't she large . . . she gave me such a charge."

"Jazzbo" Depew (Phil Gordon) makes Jethrine weak

in the knees. *Courtesy of Phil Gordon*

The Hillbillies unite in "The Legend of the Beverly
Hillbillies." *Photographs by Steve Cox*

times a day. My skin was raw and all broken out. I said, "Hey, I'm not gonna do it." We switched the schedule, and it worked better and the character was fun. And then Paul kind of killed her off, I guess.

Any time you can play things other than yourself, it's fun. Many men playing women find it a tremendous release because it's a chance to use your imagination. I may not have done it well, but I was exercising my creative muscles, which makes it very satisfying to do.

How do you feel about Jethro now?

Jethro's dead. It was something I was glad to do. I was proud to be a part of it. Probably more proud now than then in some respects. Some of my friends call me Jethro teasingly. It's like somebody calling you a son of a bitch. If he's your friend, it's okay. If he's your enemy, it's not.

And that's the way I feel about Jethro. It doesn't bother me like it did before. Sometimes I kind of enjoy it.

I'm not interested in living in the past, or holding on to it.

Postscript

May 1993: Max changed his mind. In a peculiar little documentary-styled spoof, the cast of the Hillbillies reunited in the sixty-minute, prime-time special "The Legend of the Beverly Hillbillies." Max was once again Jethro, Donna was Elly May, and Buddy played old Jed Clampett. It was CBS's highest rating for that week, possibly because Max returned.

⇥4⇤

"So They Loaded
Up the Truck . . . "

For the season opening of the sixth year, Paul Henning seemed restless, so the idea of taking the show on the road was tossed around. Henning felt a "shot in the arm" was essential to maintain a high level of interest in the show. What would be gained from such a trip, except extra cost?

The list of advantages was extensive: the series would be infused with new creative juices; new locations would mean a bright, new experience for the cast, all of whom had been with the series since its 1962 premiere; new promotions and publicity would herald the coming of yet another new season; local publicity would be sparked; and an entirely new canvas of production values would delight the millions of viewers who continued to make "The Beverly Hillbillies" a Top 10 hit every year. All valid reasons.

As far back as the third season, there had been a notion to jet the Hillbillies off to Hawaii. Europe was discussed. Not until a few seasons later did travel plans materialize. The decision was made, and budgets were prepared. The Clampetts were packin' their bags and skedaddlin'. Only they weren't just headin' yonder. They applied for passports and were trekking overseas to England.

Jettin' off to England. *Courtesy of Paul Henning*

This was the draft: Jed has inherited an English castle in Kent, England. Drysdale persuades the reluctant Hillbillies to go to England and occupy it. Drysdale's secret purpose is to accompany them and become a big-time operator in English banking circles, but Jethro unintentionally complicates his task. The marquess who bequeathed the castle is "deceased," and Dr. Granny is determined to cure whatever "decease" the marquess was stricken with.

Jethro accumulates a lavish array of Elizabethan costumes that he thinks are the proper English attire for visiting hillbillies. He wants Granny to be his oaf, and he gives Jed the noble title Earl of Clampett.

These were the first episodes of "The Beverly Hillbillies" to be shot outside Hollywood. The cast and key production personnel (nearly fifty in all) assembled in London in the early part of July 1967 and filmed from July 17 to July 21 at the stately, majestic Penshurst Castle near Tunbridge, Kent. The monstrous, 600-year-old castle had been built by Sir John de Pulteney and was the home of Lord de l'Isle. It was loaded with historical significance: in the early 1500s, King Henry VIII dined there and later beheaded his host and assumed ownership of the castle. Edward IV had dined on the castle's trestle tables—the only surviving examples of their kind—after his victory in the Wars of the Roses.

The story was perfect for the Hillbillies: Jed had just inherited the castle and the new taste of foreign customs was a perfect vehicle for new gags. Jethro was in his outlandish knight's armor, ravin' to capture a dragon that Granny was gonna fricassee. A second War of the Roses erupted between the Clampetts and the neighboring castle dwellers.

A spirited Elly May was doin' her "damsel in distress" act from the lofty tower high above the ancient castle in search of a knight in armor. The tower Donna Douglas had to climb for these episodes was reached by a trapdoor, which hadn't been opened for so many years that it was stuck. After a slight delay, the crew pounded the door heavily and finally forced it open. "Donna was

The cast on the grounds of Penshurst Castle in England.
Courtesy of Personality Photos, Inc. CBS/Fox Video

The Beverly Hillbillies

William Tell he's not: Jethro aims for the fruit on the head of the Hillbillies' English servant, Faversham (Richard Caldicot). *Courtesy of Filmways*

Granny thinks the War of the Roses is on betwixt the Clampetts and the residents of the neighboring castle. *CBS/Fox Video*

The Hillbilly Brits dance a jig upon their arrival in the United Kingdom in 1967.
Courtesy of Paul Henning

absolutely petrified up in that tower," says Nancy Kulp. "Who could blame her? It was scary."

Granny was temporarily thwarted from her doctorin' by a British customs inspector who confiscated her medical bag and its contents of wonder drugs: buckeye, snakewort, dogbane, horsemint, newt eyes, and cat hair. And as for Jed, well, he just tagged along as usual, just reckoning with things he knew nothing of.

Filming went smoothly, and the international episodes aired in succession at the beginning of the season. Not being on the soundstage did cause some distractions. Many details had to be carefully planned for the shooting, but much of the credit went to production manager George King, who was "a genius in his field," according to Paul Henning. Such details as transporting the truck, finding suitable grounds for filming, and renting the castle were arranged.

The cast bedded in London's elegant Dorchester hotel because the neighboring counties only had one inn, and it had only six rooms—not enough to accommodate the entire entourage.

"It was about an hour and a half to two hours' ride to location every day," says Joe Depew. "But Irene spent a few nights in the inn so she wouldn't have to worry about getting up so early to get to the location."

Every morning, the cast awoke while it was still dark and readied for the day's shooting. They passed each other in the lobby while grouping in taxis and limousines to be driven to the castle. Buddy Ebsen arrived a few days late for the filming because he was competing in a race with his catamaran. When he finally made it, he arrived by a helicopter that landed right on the castle grounds.

The cast and crew were warned: the British authorities requested that filming around London take place early in the morning to avoid crowds and traffic congestion. Still, there were problems.

"We were mobbed. We were shooting all over the city in costume and with the truck," Depew remembers. "We were shooting in front of Buckingham Palace, and not only were the tourists there to see the changing of the guard and all that jazz, but we had the English, too. My God, there were literally a thousand people around us. The cops, or bobbies they call 'em, were mad as hell at us. I'd often heard they are very polite, which they normally were. But they used some of the King's English, I'll tell you that. We had to get outta there."

The filming, although mobbed with fans and onlookers, ran on schedule, and the story line seemed well received by the public as the new season of Hillbilly antics got under way. The venture was such a success that for the seventh season, in 1968, Filmways decided to take the Hillbillies back to England to launch the second consecutive season opening in Europe. Key members of the production crew, cast, and writers returned to London on July 22 to begin filming four new episodes during their three-week stay. What they hadn't planned on was nearly twenty straight days of downpour. The constant rain nearly ruined the whole trip. But the fans still turned out in droves. Again, the Hillbilly Brits were welcomed with a spot of tea and crumpets.

Headin' fer Home

The Beverly Hillbillies had been in residence in Californy long enough, Paul Henning decided. They were a-headin' back to the hills. Ozarks, that is.

For the rhyme to fit the reason, Henning wrote a script that would force the Hillbillies back home: Granny hears the news that her nemesis, Elverna Bradshaw (Elvia Allman), has plans for her daughter's wedding. Granny bets Elverna she can get Elly a husband before the Bradshaw wedding takes place. So the Clampetts return home for the Silver Dollar City Fair with an ulterior motive—to find Elly a man.

In 1969, Henning took his show to the Missouri Ozarks to film on location in the little town of Branson. This marked a return to Henning's youthful days and memories of the Boy Scout camping experiences that eventually led to his creation of the series.

Henning had made several trips to the Ozarks and Branson since he created the show, and many of the props, situations, and ideas were coming from his observations. Now, there was an

Stepping off the plane at Lambert International Airport in St. Louis to a sea of press and fans. The cast was enroute to the Missouri Ozarks to film episodes in May 1969.

St. Louis Post-Dispatch photograph by Jim Rackwitz

opportunity for the television Hillbillies to meet the real folks from the hills. The cast spent a week in May filming at Silver Dollar City, a unique 2,000-acre tourist-development and theme park dedicated to the preservation of the arts and crafts of Ozark culture.

No mention had been made in the show that the Clampett family's home was in Missouri, however. This was mandatory. The names of several nearby cities, towns, and counties were spilled throughout the series' run, but a state was never revealed. Said Henning of this mandate: "We never identified the actual state location of the Clampett mountain home. I feel just as strongly now as I did in the beginning of the show that it would be a mistake to limit the imagination of the viewer in any way. It's my

The Beverly Hillbillies

belief that millions of loyal viewers believe that the Clampetts come direct from their own 'neck of the woods' and that in some measure adds to their enjoyment of the show."

Henning remembers that letters revealing a feeling of great affection and kinship came from every state with a heritage of "hardy mountain people." He told the press while filming: "Heck, I grew up in Independence, Missouri, and I'd like to feel they come from the Missouri Ozarks. That's where I first saw the real hill people when I was a boy. But the show has long since become the emotional property of the viewers, and I don't intend to slight a single one of them. We'll be in the beautiful state of Missouri, but as far as the show goes, it'll be Anywhere, USA."

For this Ozark trip, a special task force of thirty-two highly trained crew—with the cast, of course—accompanied Henning. The group included head cameraman Harry Wolf and his crew of three, production manager George King, a script supervisor, a cost accountant, the sound engineer, a key grip, a dolly grip, a gaffer,

Billboard advertisement for "The Beverly Hillbillies" on Interstate 44 (formerly Route 66) in Missouri.

Author's collection

Buddy and Irene studyin' up on their lines.
Courtesy of Silver Dollar City

Blacksmith Shad Heller and Donna Douglas become
Ozark pals. *Courtesy of Silver Dollar City*

A Confederate thru 'n' thru, Granny aims at them
Yankees. *Courtesy of Silver Dollar City*

Real Ozark hillbilly Chick Allen listens to one of
Irene's show-business squawks.
Courtesy of Silver Dollar City

Real Granny meets a reel Granny: Ethel Huffman, the lye soap maker at Silver Dollar City, chats with Irene.
Courtesy of Silver Dollar City

the property master, the film editor, two drivers, and makeup and costume assistants. This put additional costs over regular studio production close to $2,500 per person. A little project it was not, as more individuals went to Missouri than to England.

In addition, a group of Hollywood press correspondents accompanied the Beverly Hillbillies on their flight from Los Angeles to St. Louis and on the smaller chartered plane from St. Louis to Springfield, Missouri. Other press and television reporters, photographers, and interviewers converged on Silver Dollar City from all over the Midwest to cover the production.

The Ozark episodes, directed by supervising film editor Bob Leeds in the absence of an ailing Joe Depew, even drew viewers from neighboring states to witness the filming. Hundreds of tourists watched the action and talked to the stars or got autographs from behind police barricades.

The idea to film in the Ozarks originated in a letter to Paul Henning from Don Richardson, then the press and publicity agent for Silver Dollar City.

Master woodcarver Pete Engler receives compliments from Nancy Kulp and Buddy Ebsen, who observe his work at Silver Dollar City. *Courtesy of Silver Dollar City*

"I wrote Paul in 1965 and gave him an idea what this place was like," Richardson said of the wooded Ozarks park. "Paul called me and told me that he'd like to visit the place sometime and I thought, 'Yeah, yeah. Maybe sometime, only he's probably too busy.' I didn't really think he'd do it. Then I got a call from Kansas City one day. It was Paul immediately wanting to visit and asking, 'Where do I go from here?'"

Richardson helped make arrangements for the cast and crew in southern Missouri. They stayed at the Rock Lane Lodge while filming at the Silver Dollar City Hotel, the candle-making shop, the blacksmith shop, and the woodcarvers' shop, among other locations in the park. The inside set for the Silver Dollar City Hotel was replicated on the sound stage back in Hollywood, where more scenes were shot.

Among the cast were local people from the park—some were performers already—like fiddler Slim Wilson, who was made up to be a 100-year-old man in one scene, and Lloyd "Shad" Heller, an actor and blacksmith. (Heller, who subsequently made appear-

The Beverly Hillbillies

Reporter Bob Hicks interviews Nancy Kulp at Silver
Dollar City. The media converged on Missouri while
the Hillbillies filmed there.
Courtesy of Silver Dollar City

ances in four more episodes shot in Hollywood that season, also
had a role in the reunion movie airing 1981 on CBS.) Others par-
ticipating in the episodes were local arts and crafts experts like
Grannie Ethel Huffman, the lye soap maker, and master woodcarver Pete Engler.

Today, Branson, Missouri, with Silver Dollar City within, is the
Midwest's largest tourist mecca, enticing unequaled crowds during
the summer season. Some say that nearby Nashville is trying to
bury Branson. As of 1992, Branson became the number-one bus
destination in the country.

There are nearly as many celebrity theaters as hotels. Besides
the Grand Palace—owned in a joint venture by Silver Dollar City
and Kenny Rogers—celebrity theaters are owned by Roy Clark,
Andy Williams, Mel Tillis, Boxcar Willie, Mickey Gilley, Wayne
Newton, Ray Stevens, and the Osmonds. In 1993, Tony Orlando
and Bobby Vinton opened showplaces, also. These intimate showplaces have all been a success, and their stellar lineups are nothing

short of Las Vegas excellence . . . only countrified. "60 Minutes" recently called Branson "the hot new Nashville" and pointed out that "The Beverly Hillbillies" provided Branson with its primary national exposure. The reruns haven't hurt, either.

New York, the Capitol, and More

Directly after filming in the Ozarks, the Hillbillies tangled with Phil Silvers in two episodes shot in and around Manhattan. Silvers played Shifty Shafer, better known to the Clampetts as "Honest John," and, of course, they fall for his stories hook, line, and vittle. Shifty interests Jed in purchasing some "choice" pieces of New York property, which he just so happens to have on sale:

Central Park

SHIFTY: I'm willing to sell it to you at a sacrifice.
JED: It belongs to you, does it?
SHIFTY: Left to me by my late, lamented uncle—Sam Central.

Staten Island Ferry

JED: Why, you own this boat?
SHIFTY: Picked it up last month from my friend Alexander Staten.

Brooklyn Bridge

SHIFTY: Have you ever thought of owning your own bridge?
JED: No, sir.
SHIFTY: I have a bridge that I picked up at an auction last week from the estate of Oscar Brooklyn.

In a hilarious surprise cameo appearance, the Hillbillies meet up with an Irish cop in Central Park, played by Sammy Davis, Jr., who swings his nightstick and spouts an accent that a leprechaun would be proud of.

The Clampetts' final travels came in their ninth and final season when they jetted to Washington, D.C., to help the President fight the nation's pollution problem.

The two Washington episodes take the troupe to such sites as the Lincoln Memorial, Washington Monument, the Capitol, Dulles International Airport, Lafayette Park, the Smithsonian Institution's National Zoological Park, the Pentagon, and the Supreme Court building.

Jed and his family, concerned about the continuing menace of smog, want to give their money—now $95 million—to the President to help solve the problem. Drysdale, frantically trying to keep the Clampetts and their millions at home, employs the services of master impressionist Rich Little, who impersonates President Nixon in an effort to convince the family that it won't be necessary

Goin' to meet the President. *Courtesy of Personality Photos, Inc.*

No one could remember what the hell Irene was doing here. The recycling craze, perhaps? *Courtesy of Paul Henning*

for them to make the trip. He's a little *too* successful: the Hillbillies want to talk more with the President, so they pack their bags and head for the nation's capital. Phil Silvers rejoins them as Honest John—as only Phil Silvers can do. He tries to intercept the Clampett fortune before it reaches the President.

On the last day of the filming in Washington, the cast (still in makeup and costume) was given a personal tour of the White

House and Senate chambers by Senator Barry Goldwater. Heads turned that day.

Later that evening, they visited Walter Reed Army Hospital and participated in the annual spring festival entertainment for more than four hundred soldiers who had just returned from Vietnam. The program took place in the hospital's Red Cross Auditorium, and the Hillbillies were introduced by Major General Glenn J. Collins, Commander of the Walter Reed Army Medical Center.

In 1964, before the cast started filming outside Hollywood, three of its members went on tour to capitalize on their characters' extreme popularity. Irene Ryan, Donna Douglas, and Max Baer started a seventeen-day coast-to-coast personal appearance tour of eighteen cities that began on May 15 with a performance at the Cow Palace in San Francisco. They rehearsed and broke in an act during a pretour two-night stand in Tucson, Arizona, on May 9 and 10. Afterward, their schedule took them to Long Beach, California; Fort Wayne, Indiana; St. Louis; Dallas; Fort Worth; Houston; Pittsburgh; Chicago; Minneapolis; St. Paul; Sioux Falls, South Dakota; Des Moines; Charlotte, North Carolina; Baltimore; Philadelphia; Cleveland; and Milwaukee.

On the same bill were Spike Jones and Helen Grayco with the City Slickers, the Good Time Singers, the comedy act of Homer and Jethro, dancers known as the Maldonados, Yonely the musical humorist, and the Rudenko Brothers, a troupe of jugglers.

After the exhausting tour, Irene Ryan joined Donald O'Connor in a four-week engagement that began June 9 at the Sahara Hotel in Las Vegas to perform her single act, which won rave reviews on tour in the United States and on the Tivoli circuit in Australia. During the acclaimed one-woman show, Irene performed her "Granny Strip." She opened her show in costume as Granny and performed some bits in character, then she abruptly stripped down to versatile actress and comedienne Irene Ryan, dressed in a sequined dress, while a burlesque striptease theme resounded throughout the nightclub.

Kindly Droppin' In

In the nine prime-time years that the Hillbillies resided in the hills of Beverly, where movie stars and socialites shine, Jed, Granny, and the gang played host to many of the biggest celebrities in town. The show was such a hit that many of the area's most talented performers were "happy as an itchy pig rubbin' hisself against a rail fence" to land a guest spot on it.

"We not only had guest stars on the show occasionally, but we had all the big ones stopping by the set just to watch the filming or just say 'Hi,'" says actor Phil Gordon, who played Jasper "Jazzbo" Depew early in the series. "Our set wasn't completely closed, so people like Lucille Ball, Phyllis Diller, people from the 'Addams Family' cast, Ricky Nelson, Minnie Pearl, and bunches of country and western stars loved to drop by."

Some actors, like Raymond Massey, were so anxious for a guest shot or even a cameo appearance that they sent kind notes to Paul Henning with more than subtle hints that they'd love to work for him. When the show hit hard, Spike Jones enthusiastically offered his talents as musical director. Back then, it was like today's version

John Wayne saddled up with the Hillbillies for an episode. *Courtesy of Joe Depew*

of supplying a "guest voice" on "The Simpsons." An episode of "Hillbillies" was the thing to do.

There were some, like Glen Campbell, whom Paul Henning pursued. Henning and another writer prepared a full script on spec, hoping the young country singer might appear on the show. Campbell's manager, Nick Sevano, never delivered Paul Henning's persistent solicitations because he thought the show was beneath his client. The script was quickly rewritten and Pat Boone was

Sammy Davis, Jr., played an Irish cop in one of the New York episodes. *Courtesy of Paul Henning*

Soupy Sales is Mrs. Drysdale's nephew, Lance Bradford, who arrives home from the air force and interests Jethro in the service. *Viacom*

The Beverly Hillbillies

substituted. Another script idea had the Hillbillies seeing an old Shirley Temple film, *Captain January*, in which Buddy Ebsen danced with her. Of course the Hillbillies, charmed by her cuteness, would still think of her as a six-year-old moppet. The former actress was approached about appearing on the show, but declined and the idea was dropped.

Sharon Tate, who is more famous for her savage murder by the Charles Manson gang in the late sixties than for her acting, appeared in many episodes as Janet Trego, one of the secretarial pool at the Commerce Bank. Most of the time she donned a black wig for the role.

"When we first got her she couldn't even walk through the door convincingly," said Joe Depew. "She was very amateurish. It was hard for her to read a line. Then she went to [acting] school, and she learned a lot. She was a very pleasant girl and extremely beautiful . . . a real tragedy."

Max Baer, who dated Tate during the series,

The cast that never was. Actress Sharon Tate (left) was originally cast as the third daughter in TV's "Petticoat Junction." Just before the series started, however, *Playboy* published nude photos that Tate had posed for prior to receiving the role. Immediately, Filmways released her from her contract, fearing scandal and negative publicity. Pictured with Tate are Bea Benaderet, Linda Kaye Henning, and Pat Woodall. *Courtesy of Paul Henning*

Roy Clark, in drag, for his television acting debut. *Courtesy of Filmways*

Phil Silvers plays a con artist (what else?) who sells Jed several choice pieces of land. (Watch where you put that hand, Max!) *Courtesy of Filmways*

Kindly Droppin' In (continued)

comments: "She was a lovely girl, but I never got that close to her."

Before he played Archie Bunker's son-in-law, "Meathead," on "All in the Family" or started his career as a film director, Rob Reiner frequented sitcoms such as "Gomer Pyle, U.S.M.C." and "Hillbillies" as a long-haired, bearded hippie: "I was a professional hippy on television in the sixties," Reiner said in an interview recently. "I was hired because the real hippies were always stoned and couldn't remember their lines. I could remember my lines."

Of course, no sitcom of the sixties was complete without those regular character actors Burt Mustin, Lyle Talbot, Kathleen Freeman, Elvia Allman, John McGiver, Olan Soule, Herb Vigran, Charles Lane, Mary Wickes, Fred Clark, and Milton Frome. The Hillbillies didn't forget them, nor did they shun the likes of

Eddie Albert	Jim Backus
Lola Albright	Mel Blanc

Lowell Reddlings Farquhar (Charlie Ruggles) doesn't seem at all disturbed by Jed's poker hand—four aces—because he's holding a straight flush in the episode "Mrs. Drysdale's Father."

Courtesy of Filmways

Pat Boone	June Lockhart
Foster Brooks	Paul Lynde
Edgar Buchanan	Meredith MacRae
Sebastian Cabot	Ralph Morgan
John Carradine	Julie Newmar
Ted Cassidy	Louis Nye
Roy Clark	Rob Reiner
Hans Conried	Don Rickles
Ellen Corby	Hayden Rorke
Wally Cox	Charlie Ruggles
Sammy Davis, Jr.	Soupy Sales
Richard Deacon	Natalie Schafer
Rosemary DeCamp	Phil Silvers
Leo Durocher	Gloria Swanson
Eva Gabor	Arthur Treacher
Henry Gibson	John Wayne
Hedda Hopper	Jesse White
Bernie Kopell	Paul Winchell
Rich Little	

Of all the guests visiting the Clampett domain, the most memorable for the cast was probably John Wayne, who made a cameo appearance in "The Indians Are Coming."

"We wrote that bit in for him because Buddy was good friends with the Duke, so Buddy called him and asked him to appear," says Paul Henning, an unabashed fan of the actor. "Duke said he liked our show and would be glad to do it. It was such a quick bit, though, I don't even think they bothered with makeup for him."

It was Lester Flatt and Earl Scruggs who played the guitar instrumentals for the show's theme song, "The Ballad of Jed Clampett," and together they appeared in several "Hillbillies" episodes as themselves. Flatt and Scruggs met when each joined the band of the "father of bluegrass music," Bill Monroe, back in the 1940s. In 1948 they ventured out and created their own

The Beverly Hillbillies

Bluegrass legends Lester Flatt and Earl Scruggs entertain the folks in the Clampett's makeshift cabin built on the mansion grounds. *CBS/Fox Video*

sound, then formed the enormously popular Foggy Mountain Boys. Until they broke up in 1969, Flatt and Scruggs released many hit singles and albums, several of which included their version of "The Ballad of Jed Clampett." In 1967, their "Foggy Mountain Breakdown" became, famous as "The Theme from *Bonnie and Clyde.*"

As neither of the famed musicians could act, their dialogue was minimal. They were there for their singing. The catchy little country tune "Pearl, Pearl, Pearl" ("don't give yer love to Earl"), written by Paul Henning, was a cute love ballad Flatt and Scruggs

chimed to Cousin Pearl, hoping to woo her into choosing one of them for a husband.

Nancy Kulp remembered one of her favorite guest stars with fondness. He was the endearing lead of TV's "Mr. Peepers," Wally Cox, who played

Wally Cox plays P. Casper Biddle, the gentle leader of the Biddle Bird-watchers Society of Beverly Hills. Jane Hathaway is the flockmaster in search of the condor. *Courtesy of Personality Photos, Inc.*

Kindly Droppin' In (continued)

Professor Bittle, a gentle bird-watcher—not unlike Cox's true persona, Kulp said. In her extensive scenes with Cox in two "Hillbillies" episodes, Kulp reverted to the bird-watching Pamela Livingston she had played on "The Bob Cummings Show."

"He was a very gentle, soft-spoken man," Kulp said. "It was hard not to like Wally. Everyone was fond of him. One year, he came to my house for Thanksgiving on a motorcycle with his daughter sitting right behind him."

For the most unique of all guest shots, the award goes to Gloria Swanson, the silent-screen queen who was pulled out of retirement to star in the motion picture classic *Sunset Boulevard* in 1950. For Swanson, television appearances were a rarity, but she agreed to this one, in which she played herself. She admitted to reporters that playing herself made her "a bit nervous," but at $2,500 for less than three days' work, she coped. In fact, Swanson might have been the highest-paid guest star the show ever had.

In this nostalgic episode, Jed is stunned to find out that Swanson is auctioning off some of her personal belongings for a charity benefit. When many of her things are hauled out of the house, Jed thinks she's destitute, tossed out by an ungrateful Hollywood. He decides to revitalize her career by starring her in a new film for the motion picture studio he has just purchased.

"Gloria Swanson was nice to work with, a thorough pro," says Henning.

"Everyone was very much in awe," remembered Nancy Kulp. "Most of the time, she worked with me. I remember on the set she kept telling me not to eat white sugar. She was very interested in nutrition and lived to a ripe old age; she had a very stringent diet, and everything had to be natural. She said that white sugar was poisoning the world. I don't want to ridicule her, though; that was her thing. In fact . . . I don't eat much white sugar."

When Phil Silvers joined the cast as Shifty Shafer, the rule of obeying the script verbatim was tossed aside for the week. "That was rare," Henning points out, "but Phil couldn't read a script cold. He was terrible. But when he gets on, there's nobody better. Nobody. He kept using a different line each take, but each one was a classic. We always looked forward to having him on the show."

Former silent film star Gloria Swanson came out of retirement to appear as herself on "The Beverly Hillbillies." *Courtesy of Personality Photos, Inc.*

The Beverly Hillbillies

Them Thar 'billies

Jed explained how it happened in only one episode: "You see, Granny was honin' fer some gopher gravy.

"I went down t' the slew to shoot one. But jus' as I cut loose, that little varmint skedaddled an' oil come a oozin' outta that slew jus' like sorghum out of a leaky hog-trough. That's how I made my fortune."

Everyone, of course, knows the tale. It's told in the opening montage of the show pretty near every time you watch: Jed joins the millionaire league and files for California residency. By the ninth season, he's a member of the Fortune 500 with a bank account that has swelled to $95 million. And yet, he remains a hillbilly.

The Jed Clampett conglomeration hailed from Cass County in the Ozarks. (Some towns in Cass County included Bug Tussel, Possum Trot, and Mincy.) Theirs was a nontraditional ensemble as television families went back then.

Commonly, the four of them were known as the Clampett family, although only two of them were Clampetts, Jed and Elly May. Let's clarify something else: despite popular belief, Granny was *not* Jed's mother, and Jethro and Elly May were *not* brother and sister.

The bloodline was this: widower Jed Clampett and widow Pearl Bodine were first blood cousins, which made Jed's daughter, Elly May, and Pearl's boy, Jethro, second cousins. Granny (real name Daisy Moses) was Jed's mother-in-law. (The former Rose Ellen Moses, Granny's daughter who married Jed, was mentioned only once.) Got it?

Then what would Granny be to Jethro? They're not related (only by marriage). Maybe that's why Granny had more venom for Jethro than for her only spinster granddaughter, Elly May.

Paul Henning created these characters either by basing them on people he knew or by combining traits of those who had impressed him in one way or another over the years. Jed Clampett reminded Henning of a kindly, strong, and wise hillbilly man he had known as a child, while Milburn Drysdale was mostly based on an unscrupulous, coldhearted banker Henning had once known in the Midwest. Henning's five sisters became the names of Elly's chickens: Drusilla, Florence, Rosie, Viola, and Lillie. Henning's kin, his friends and associates, and the cast and crew never knew when their own names might wind up as characters on the next week's show. Once, Henning contacted an old schoolmate and asked if he could use his wife's maiden name on the show. The friend agreed, Henning paid her $100, and "Essiebelle Crick" was created. Henning warned her that the character was a hillbilly girl whom Jethro remembered as a beauty, but who, it turns out, has grown obese since the last time he saw her. The former Miss Crick agreed nonetheless.

These characters were rich in background because Henning drew not only from his own experiences but because he devoured such books on Ozark culture as *Ozark Superstitions* and *Ozark Mountain Folk* by Vance Randolph and several Otto Rayburn books. The meticulous producer unearthed many back issues of *Ozark Guide* magazines that aided his research and occasionally provided story concepts. So authentic were his Hillbillies that Pat Buttram, TV's Mr. Haney from "Green Acres," once said: "Where I come from, 'The Beverly Hillbillies' is considered a documentary."

Henning read the frequent letters he

An early family portrait. *Courtesy of Personality Photos, Inc.*

received and the printed editorials complaining that his Hillbillies were too ignorant. Some viewers complained that *nowhere* in the United States, in this civilized age, could there be such people. "What eased the sting was the tens of thousands of letters and cards that came in," Henning told the press in 1965. "They were

thank yous for making the Hillbillies clean, decent, God-fearing people. [The Hillbillies] were honest, sincere people with good virtues—only they lacked knowledge of the sophisticated world."

TV Guide decided to put the show to a test. The magazine dispatched a writer into the deep woods of Three Brothers, Arkansas. There, a reporter found and interviewed a twenty-two-year-old "gen-u-wine authentic" Ozark mountainer, as Mr. Haney might say. His name was Junior Cobb, and he was recruited to give his opinion of the show and its characters.

The nearest television was four miles from Cobb's small, self-built, pasteboard-wall 20' × 20' cabin. Cobb whittled wooden souvenir-stand figurines that packed the pockets of his overalls with $85 a month to support his wife and infant daughter. His education was minimal, and he was unaware of any written criticism of the show, but he offered up his opinion after watching a few half hours: "Theys got a good, funny pergr'm . . . that Granny, she's zackly like my Gran'ma McCarty." His only objection concerned a Hillbilly-cast Winston cigarette commercial during the break: "It just don't seem rot for Jad to light up a cig-ret like he did. Seems as how it'd be better if he had *rolled-up* one."

Cobb lived on the other end of the state from fellow Arky Bill Clinton, who's been accused of being a bit "hillbilly." "Saturday Night Live" had its roast combining Clinton and "The Beverly Hillbillies."

Spoofing the presidential debates in late '92, moderator Sam Donaldson (played by Kevin Nealon) questioned Bill Clinton (Phil Hartman), George Bush, and Ross Perot (both played by Dana Carvey):

Sam Donaldson: Governor Clinton, let's be frank. You're running for President, yet your only experience has been as the governor of a small, backwoods state with a population of drunken hillbillies riding around in pickup trucks. The main streets of your capital city, Little Rock, are something out of Little Abner, with buxom under-aged girls in cutoff denims prancing around in front of Jethro . . . while corncob-pipe-smoking, shotgun-toting grannies fire indiscriminately at runaway hogs.

Bill Clinton: I'm sorry, Sam . . . do you have a question?

Sam Donaldson: My question is, How can you stand it? Don't you lose your mind living down there?

Bill Clinton: I'm tired of the Bush campaign trying to portray my state as some primitive Third World country. Fact is, Arkansas *did* have a long way to go, but we've made progress. When I started as governor, we were fiftieth in adult literacy. And last year, I'm proud to say we shot ahead a' Mississippi. We're forty-nine and we're closin' in fast on Alabama! Watch out, Alabama! We gotcher number!

George Bush: Two years ago I went on a fishing trip in Arkansas with Baker, Fitzwater, Quayle, myself. It was fun, but we were chased and assaulted by a couple of inbred mountain people. . . . Now, I was sworn to secrecy as to those events, but suffice to say they felt that Dan Quayle, and I quote, "sure had a perdy mouth."

Ross Perot: Can I jump in here? Now, why are we talkin' about Arkansas? Hell ever'body knows all they got down there are a bunch a ignorant, inbred crackers. Peckerwoods. Catch me? Can we talk about deficit? While we been jabberin' here, our deficit has increased by a half-million dollars. That's enough to buy a still and a new outhouse for every family in Little Rock.

→5←
"Pity-full...Piiiiiity-full"

Granny had gone to her reward. Jed had divided up his fortune between Jethro and Elly May; the two younguns invested in their respective interests: Jethro was the owner and head producer of Mammoth (motion picture) Studios; Elly May owned a zoo. Mr. Drysdale had gone to the great mint in the sky, while Jane Hathaway—still *Miss* Jane—was now a Washington, D.C., "career girl" working for the government. Jed sold his mansion in Beverly Hills and moved back to the cabin where it all started—only he added onto the cabin for a little more space.

This was the opening sequence of the made-for-television movie *The Return of The Beverly Hillbillies*, which updated audiences on the lives of the Clampetts in 1981. Creator Paul Henning had reassembled its stars, Buddy Ebsen, Nancy Kulp, and Donna Douglas. Max Baer, however, did not wish to return to the show that boosted him to fame. Those three characters—Jed, Elly May, and Miss Jane—were the only remnants of the original show. The return lost more than the characters; it lost the original humor that made the show so popular.

Henning did, however, write the show, while Bob Leeds, an occasional director on the original show, directed. (Leeds was then in the process of getting divorced from Donna Douglas.) Actors Shad Heller and Shug Fisher, who appeared in several episodes in the late sixties also had roles in the two-hour movie. Earl Scruggs flew in from Tennessee to contribute some guitar picking, but his old bluegrass partner of many years, Lester Flatt, had died in 1979.

Factors contributing to the production's failure were many. For Donna Douglas, it was the movie's lack of nostalgia. "If you think about it," she says, "it had none of the original premises. No roots. The house was gone, the car was gone. No bank, Drysdale was not there, and the only cast members from the original were me, Buddy, and Nancy. The anchors were just not there."

There were reasons other than nostalgia in collecting the actors again for this TV movie. As Henning explains, the main one was financial; unfortunately, the movie did not prove lucrative. Rebuilding the original sets would have been costly, so Henning wrote the movie around Jed's cabin back in the hills.

"It was purely a business enterprise. Purely a chance to make some money," Henning says. "A fellow by the name of Ron Beckman, who had been in charge of contracts at the old studio, came to see me and said he thought we could reap a financial harvest by having the Hillbillies get together again. We all succumbed to the possibility of making money and keeping money. Capital gains as it were. Money was the incentive."

But Henning was not in the best of health at the time. "I had started taking a blood pressure depressant to hold my blood pressure down, which was dangerously high," he explains. "I didn't want to have a stroke. I took four of these pills a day and it did indeed lower the blood pressure, but it also lowered my awareness. I called it a pharmaceutical lobotomy."

To complicate matters, just when Henning sat down with the cast and the read-throughs proved the script was not up to the old Hillbilly standards, a Writers Guild strike was called. He could not alter the script by any means. Henning did not have the time to rewrite the whole script, so the story remained much the same, to the disappointment of those involved, especially Henning, one of television's most talented comedy constructors.

Comedienne Imogene Coca stars as Granny's 104-year-old maw, in the ill-fated TV reunion flick. *Courtesy of Paul Henning*

"I take full responsibility for the failure of *The Return of the Beverly Hillbillies*," says its creator. "It was a bad script and I knew it was a bad script and when it came time to rewrite it, the Writers Guild went on strike. I was helpless, 'between a rock and a hard place,' as a hillbilly would say."

Once again, Buddy Ebsen applied a mustache and dusted off the torn hat and tan jacket to spout a "Well, Doggies!" for the fans. Donna Douglas fit right back into rope-tied jeans to hug the critters. The cast also included Imogene Coca as Granny's 104-

year-old maw. Werner Klemperer, who starred in "Hogan's Heroes" as the inept German colonel Klink, played C. D. Medford, a government bureaucrat who almost marries Jane Hathaway. Actor Ray Young, who, at a distance, looked similar to Max Baer, filled in for Jethro; Linda Kaye Henning played the role of Jethro Bodine's secretary at the motion picture studio.

"We missed Granny terribly," said Shad Heller. "And Max was a loss, too. He originally said yes to Paul when he was approached about the part. He kept saying yes, but when it got close to filming, Paul could not get hold of Max. He was dodging Paul. Finally, Paul sent someone to see Max, and Max refused the part at the last minute, so they found this other guy who looked a little like Jethro, but wasn't a seasoned actor. He did what he could."

Baer later explained: "I was twenty years older. I don't think it would have worked for me." Baer tried to shy away from his identification with the role that most viewers and, unfortunately, most casting directors, had. "I felt trapped in that part from the beginning. I felt that way when I first did it. Just like Archie Bunker. Carroll O'Connor will always be Archie Bunker."

Baer was not the only original cast member to feel the difference. "It wasn't the same," Nancy Kulp said. "At first I fought the idea of doing the movie. Finally, Paul called and wanted to meet with me, and it was like a scene out of *The Godfather*; it was pouring rain on a really dark day, and I remember Paul and I getting together, both of us holding up umbrellas. He pleaded with me, 'I'd really like you to be in this movie, Nancy.'

"It was very difficult," Kulp says. "I never thought Imogene Coca was good casting, but they did and I wasn't going to say anything. Director Bob Leeds used these idiotic shots, many over-the-shoulder shots that don't lend themselves to comedy. It was atrocious. But I must say it was good to get back together with some of the people from the show. I just wish it would have turned out better, that's all."

The plot was simple—unlike some of the early vintage Hillbilly episodes, which sometimes contained a network of subplots all being led down the road to one hilarious upshot.

Miss Hathaway and her associate, C. D. Medford, fly from Washington on special assignment from the President to get a sampling of Granny's white lightnin'. Miss Hathaway believed this potent concoction would eradicate the energy crisis for good. Upon her return to the hills, she is reunited with the Clampett patriarch—and with several of Granny's empty jugs of white lightnin'. The only living soul who knows the recipe is Granny's 104-

Miss Jane gets her man—almost. Werner Klemperer and Nancy Kulp costar in *The Return of the Beverly Hillbillies. Courtesy of Paul Henning*

The Beverly Hillbillies

year-old maw, who whips up a batch only for special occasions. So Miss Jane and Medford reluctantly marry, and a wingding takes place at the Clampetts' once again.

It ends up that Jed knew the marriage was not made for love, so he arranged for a substitute judge and the marriage was never valid. (Mighty bold of Jed.) The final knee-slapper: Medford accidently drank the white lightnin'.

The film was well publicized by CBS, which aired promos regularly. There were hopes for a resurgence in popularity, and the press dangled thoughts of a new series in front of viewers eyes. But was Paul Henning ready for another series?

"No. Frankly," he says, "I didn't want to get back into that glass furnace." Henning also reluctantly admits the film did not reap the harvest intended. The corn was planted too late, some think.

The film did not fare well in the ratings that October 6, 1981, on the season premiere of the CBS "Tuesday Night Movie." Moreover, this was the evening that every network interrupted its broadcast to relay the news that Egyptian President Anwar Sadat had been assassinated. A ratings booster this was not, but even without that bad news, the ratings would have put them third. A rebroadcast on "CBS Saturday Night Movie" on July 7, 1984, brought less-than-favorable ratings. Movie and television historian Leonard Maltin noted that taking "The Beverly Hillbillies" out of "comfortable retirement in TV heaven" was not a wise choice and rated the film "below average."

So this comeback for "The Beverly Hillbillies" was ventured, but not gained. Faithful watchers of the Hillbillies winced at the reunion, yet at the same time felt it was nice to set a spell with their friends once again. The Hillbillies always said, "Y'all come back now, y' hear?" . . . and they did—only the viewers didn't.

6

Laughing All the Way
to the Commerce Bank

If [The Dick Van Dyke Show] hadn't followed an unknown show named
"The Beverly Hillbillies" last year, I doubt we would be back. That little
show really took off . . . it became the country's top show and I think it
delivered us a whopping big audience. We owe a lot to that strange little
show.

—Mary Tyler Moore
TV Week, December 19, 1964

Mary Tyler Moore's statement is particularly relevant today.
Attempting to surpass the records set by "The Beverly Hillbillies" would be harder than sneakin' daylight past a rooster. Networks knew it back then. Networks know it now. In today's television race, the scrambling network heads would kill for even the Hillbillies *lowest* rating.

Before the end of the Hillbillies' first season, CBS was understandably anxious to air another show under Paul Henning's supervision. The success of his "Hillbillies" made the network greedy to play copycat and start a run of rural shows since it felt the program was starting a trend.

Henning was interested in giving actress Bea Benaderet her own show. He was quite infatuated with her talent and wanted to utilize her skill as a comedienne and versatile performer in something other than her role as Jed Clampett's Cousin Pearl, aka Maw to Jethro.

In 1963, along came "Petticoat Junction," a show that began with a concept Henning created based on his wife's memories of visiting her grandparents, who ran the Burris Hotel next to a railroad track in Eldon, Missouri. And CBS was glad of it. The program was gold in them thar Henning hills, and again the network was as thirsty as a hound-chased fox for another Henning hit. CBS President James Aubrey (sometimes known as "The Smiling Cobra") made Henning an offer that was virtually unheard of: an open time slot for *anything* he wished to put on the air—with NO pilot necessary. Henning got up from his chair, kissed the reptile on the forehead, and left the room.

He quickly fulfilled the offer by giving Aubrey "Green Acres" in 1965 (actually created by writer Jay Sommers), which incorporated "Petticoat" and "Hillbillies" into what Henning called a "cross-pollination." (Cast members from all three shows occasionally intermingled—an idea that again became popular with the

In an extrasurreal episode of "Green Acres," residents of Hooterville put on a community theater production that spoofs their country cousins, the Beverly Hillbillies. Hank Kimball (Alvy Moore) played Jed, Lisa Douglas (Eva Gabor) became Granny, and Oliver Douglas (Eddie Albert) was Jethro. *Courtesy of Alvy Moore*

Irene and Buddy were left empty-handed every
Emmy night. *Courtesy of Personality Photos, Inc.*

recent Witt-Thomas hit shows "The Golden Girls," "Empty
Nest," and "Nurses" on NBC.)

Despite the long, successful runs of Henning's creations, plus
high marks for collaborating on "Green Acres," Henning was
never recognized by his peers.

Truly recognized, that is. The show was recognized with a few
nominations, but never rewarded with an Emmy. After the show's
first season, the Academy of Television Arts and Sciences nominated Henning for Emmys for Outstanding Program Achievement
in the Field of Humor and Outstanding Writing Achievement in
Comedy (1962–63 season). Henning lost out to "The Dick Van
Dyke Show" and Carl Reiner, respectively. Twice Irene Ryan was
nominated for Outstanding Continued Performance by an Actress
in a Series, but first lost out to actress Shirley Booth, who starred
in the NBC sitcom "Hazel," and the next year to Mary Tyler
Moore from "The Dick Van Dyke Show." In 1967, Nancy Kulp

The Beverly Hillbillies

lost as Best Supporting Actress. In addition, Richard Whorf was nominated twice during his tenure as the show's director, but never won.

The Hillbillies left every Emmy show empty-handed.

"That was terrible," remembers Al Simon. "We all attended the Academy presentation that first year of the show. We didn't win anything, but I will tell you this . . . after Dick Van Dyke went up and received his Emmy, honest to God, he looked over to our table where Paul was sitting and bowed." *TV Guide* also noted the gesture: "At [the Academy] awards dinner emceed by Van Dyke, the grateful comedian turned to the 'Hillbillies' table, raised his arms above his head, bowed low, and salaamed."

It is assumed that "The Dick Van Dyke Show," which got canceled after its first year due to awful ratings, was pulled from the depths after being rescheduled to follow "The Hillbillies" on Wednesday nights. "Van Dyke" was raised to number nine in its second season and climbed to number three in its third year—still trailing "The Hillbillies" in time slot and ratings. And yet "The Dick Van Dyke Show" went on to win fifteen Emmy awards during its five seasons on TV.

After that fateful Emmy night of May 26, 1963, when the Hillbillies first went home empty-handed, Carl Reiner, creator and producer of "The Dick Van Dyke Show," sent a letter to Paul Henning expressing sincere regret that "Hillbillies" did not win an Emmy, despite its popularity, which towered over that of his own show. Moreover, Danny Thomas, top man on the "Van Dyke Show" and also a "Hillbillies" fan, sent Henning a box of cigars.

"The year that we were nominated," said Nancy Kulp, "the Hillbillies were invited to present something, but they wanted them in costume. It was very demeaning. Since then, I've walked out on the Academy. By the time I was nominated for an Emmy in '67, none of us were members of the Academy at all and I've never gone back." Nevertheless, until her death, Kulp carried a card for the Screen Actors Guild and the Motion Picture Academy.

The loss of Emmys was not the first crushing blow to the Hillbillies company. Irony surrounded the series' whole existence. The ratings were overwhelming, yet the recognition for the creator and performers by peers was near zero.

Nancy Kulp said: "As for the criticism, we finally just said, 'Screw you,' in effect. The thing that angered and infuriated us most was the lack of recognition they gave Paul for his brilliance. I think the man is a genius. And these half-baked entrepreneurs in Hollywood didn't seem to recognize that humor doesn't necessarily speak in an English accent. They were the pseudointellectuals that tried to tear us apart. At first we were very angry, then we just got used to it and kept hoping time after time that Paul would get an award."

Nonetheless, "The Beverly Hillbillies" was a powerful show with immense popularity feeding it. It was so popular, in fact, that CBS decided in the late sixties to begin airing episodes in its morning lineup. The show scored big in Great Britain, where it

---

Whuppin' the Critics

"The Beverly Hillbillies" became TV's whipping boy for critics who wanted to illustrate seemingly bad television. Paul Henning took the lashings and went about his business.

Henning has read many critical analyses of his show, and more than one college dissertation has put his characters under a microscope. It surprises Henning when the program is fitted with cultural symbolism. The show was simply meant to entertain, an essential element in most television programming.

Newsweek noted that reviewers had criticized the program, calling it "clumsy slapstick, unworthy of air time." The magazine let the show's creator defend his product. "My shows were not meant to replace anything," Henning said, "just to be one of the many facets of programming. It doesn't take a very high I.Q. to watch pro football, and look how many people do. Why go into deep analysis about it?"

There were good and bad reviews. As the show lived on, the bad got worse, and the good sweetened. Here's a sampling of the dissension:

- Jack Gould of the *New York Times* wrote in 1962: "The Beverly Hillbillies is steeped in enough twanging guitar, polka-dot gingham, deliberative drawl, prolific cousins, and rural no-think to make each half hour seem as if it contained sixty minutes. . . . Indeed there seems every likelihood that perhaps the worst of the new season's entries will be the biggest hit of the lot."
- *Saturday Review* stood up in 1963: "Valid social criticism with a Top-ten Nielsen is an absolute rarity in television. This is the true measure of the success of 'The Beverly Hillbillies'—the first of its kind."
- Rick Du Brow, writing for United Press International in the 1960s, wrote, "The show aims

was the first TV comedy show in British TV history to be given a *second* showing in the same week. The Japanese couldn't get enough of our homespun American characters, and, at its height, "Hillbillies" was broadcast in fifty-two countries. Australia was hoppin' with the Hillbillies, and the show is still revered as a rerun there.

"Humor is humor," points out Max Baer. "It's the same reason the show was popular in Greece and it played Saudi Arabia. The show was universally funny. We were very popular among the Southerners and the blacks."

"The black community absolutely loved Irene," says Granny's agent, Kingsley Colton. "If blacks would recognize her in a restaurant, they would definitely come over to say hello. And Irene loved it." Paul Henning recalled the day the cast filmed at Los Angeles International Airport and drew quite a crowd to witness

---

low and hits its target." The *New York Times Magazine* stamped it "one of the greatest sources of current dismay in half-hour television."

- The Dallas *Morning News* proclaimed: "It's corn, all right, but crisp, crunchy, and rather refreshing."

Item: The show was so successful that a porn flick was named after it. *The Beverly Thrillbillies* is the story of Head Clamper and his incestuous family, Granny, Elly May, Jef-toe, and banker Drytail.

Item: The spastic Weird Al Yankovic 1989 film *UHF* featured a computer-generated animated music video about the Hillbillies that combined the Dire Straits song "Money for Nothing" with the lyrics of "The Ballad of Jed Clampett."

Item: Consider the recent, popular TV sitcom that parallels "The Beverly Hillbillies": NBC's

"Fresh Prince of Bel Air" (complete with an explanatory opening rap theme song).

Item: In 1992, the *Associated Press* reported that in America the show was syndicated in fifty-five cities and run on TBS cable network. AP writer Frazier Moore noted, "Now on its 30th anniversary, 'The Beverly Hillbillies' remains among the funniest, most inspired of all TV comedies—and yet one that even its fans still watch down their noses . . .

"In retrospect, they seem downright progressive, those counterculture Clampetts. So was their show. Much more than gags about possum innards and fishing in the cee-ment pond, 'The Beverly Hillbillies' continues to tweak a foolish modern world that the Clampetts occupied without losing their souls. Smirk if you must, but the Clampetts look smarter with every passing season. More than ever, the joke is on the rest of us."

Buddy Ebsen: "I remember Irene had to go to the bathroom so bad during this long parade through downtown St. Louis. Finally, she made the parade stop while she ran into a Famous Barr department store and headed for the bathroom and then ran back." *Author's collection*

the number-one show being shot. "I remember there were groups and groups of black people who approached the cast and just wanted to talk to them and touch them," he says. "Many more than from the white crowd. I always thought that was interesting." (Yet only a few blacks ever appeared on the show, the most famous being Sammy Davis, Jr.) Keep in mind, many blacks in the pre–Civil Rights era could identify with the downtrodden Hillbillies in this rags-to-riches adventure. "It seemed back then, the poorer the people, the more it appealed to them," concludes Max Baer.

But the fullest extent of the rewards were in the show's multiple score in the list of top-rated programs of all time, according to the A. C. Nielsen ratings system. "The Beverly Hillbillies" has the distinction of claiming an unsurpassed *eight* individual episode entries in the list of 100 All-Time Top-Rated Programs. These eight episodes are up in the ranks of such television phenomena as the moon landing, the final M*A*S*H episode, the climactic "Who Shot J.R.?" segments on "Dallas," "Roots," *Gone With the Wind*'s television premiere and its subsequent airings, "The Thorn Birds," "The Day After," and countless highly rated Super Bowls.

The "Hillbillies" episode with the highest rating aired on January 8, 1964. "The Giant Jackrabbit" is a record-setting episode that has remained the highest-rated half-hour program, bar none, since 1960. No one from the show could ever quite figure out why this particular episode excelled, except to conclude that momentum had built and the show peaked right then.

Greeting thousands at the Houston Astrodome during the height of the show's success on prime time.

Courtesy of Buddy Ebsen

The ratings history of "The Beverly Hillbillies," out of the Top 25 prime-time network shows each year, is as follows:

Year	Rank	Rating
1962–63:	#1	36.0
1963–64:	#1	39.1
1964–65:	#12	25.6
1965–66:	#8	25.9
1966–67:	#9	23.4
1967–68:	#12	23.3
1968–69:	#10	23.5
1969–70:	#18	21.7
1970–71:	finished outside the Top 25	

The argument has been raised—especially by entertainers who didn't fare well in the ratings—that the Nielsen race is nothing short of politics. Can the ratings be trusted, and are they an accurate reflection of the viewers' taste?

In 1963, *TV Guide* tackled the matter differently and took a readers' poll, more aptly referred to as the Viewers' Poll, and asked what the people really thought. Once again, "The Beverly Hillbillies" conquered the competition. It was acclaimed the best new show of the year by more than a quarter million *TV Guide* readers. (The magazine capitalized on the program's popularity by featuring the Hillbillies on eight separate covers over the years.)

Awards, That Is! Honors, Recognition, Popularity . . .

• "The Beverly Hillbillies" won Australia's most coveted television award, the Logie, as the most popular overseas program series broadcast in Australia. Donna Douglas accepted the invitation to visit Melbourne to receive the golden statuette on behalf of the cast. The presentation took place during a charity ball on Friday, March 26, 1965, sponsored by *TV Week* magazine, which conducted the poll. In attendance were much of Austalia's officialdom, including the State Premier and Melbourne's Lord Mayor.

•Irene Ryan, who observed her fiftieth year in show business in 1967, was honored with the Genii Award by the Radio and Television Women of Southern California at the thirteenth annual Genii Award banquet at the Beverly Hilton Hotel in Beverly Hills, California, on Saturday, April 15, 1967.

•October 20, 1965, was officially proclaimed Possum Day in Beverly Hills, California. Mayor Frank Clapp saluted the Hillbillies on the steps of Beverly Hills City Hall with all the main members of the cast present to lead the festive tribute to the homely marsupial. The entree at the luncheon, by the way, was possum.

•The American Humane Society honored Donna Douglas with a special award, and stars of "The Beverly Hillbillies" and "Petticoat Junction" were cited at the annual convention of the

Australia's Logie award was presented to "The Beverly Hillbillies" as the most popular overseas program broadcast down under. Douglas accepted the award at Melbourne's Palais de Dance. Here she is with Australian Logie winner Jimmy Hannan. *Courtesy of TV Week*

In 1989, Nancy Kulp hosted a television retrospective about "The Hillbillies" for Seattle's KTZZ-TV. *Photograph by Tom Wallace*

Los Angeles metropolitan district of the California Federation of Women's Clubs. Douglas was cited for "consistently demonstrating kindness and compassion for a wide assortment of living 'critters' and making a valuable contribution to the humane cause." She received the honor at the fourteenth annual Patsy award ceremonies of the American Humane Association.

• During her Hawaiian vacation, notes a 1967 CBS press release, Irene Ryan was crowned "Queen of Kauai," an honor that was the realization of a lifelong ambition for the wispy little actress. "I always wanted to be the queen of something—anything," said Ryan, "but with a figure that reads 21 from top to bottom, I never felt I had a chance against the usual 36-23-36 competition."

The Beverly Hillbillies

• The "Show Me" state of Missouri showed Paul Henning what it thought of him with a special Distinguished Native Son award created for the producer by then governor Warren E. Hearnes. Mrs. Hearnes made the presentation in May 1969, when Henning took his Hillbillies to the Missouri Ozarks to film parts of five episodes that were shown throughout the season.

• At a press reception concluding a week of filming "The Beverly Hillbillies" in Washington, D.C., a certificate of appreciation from the United States Coast Guard was given to Buddy Ebsen for "notable services" in the production of a series of television films on proper boating. Ebsen, a yachtsman of national prominence and winner of several major boating competitions, served with the Coast Guard in World War II. Rear Admiral J. J. McClelland presented the award, which took place in the studios of WTOP-TV, a CBS affiliate in Washington, D.C.

• Irene Ryan was honored as Woman of the Year (1968) by the National Father's Day Committee at the annual Father of the Year

The Movieland Wax Museum exhibit in Buena Park, California. *Courtesy of Movieland Wax Museum*

The Hillbillies facilitate Uncle Sam's reminder to file your tax returns.

Photograph by Gabi Rona

Awards Luncheon held at the Waldorf-Astoria Hotel in New York. The citation noted that "besides being active in the entertainment world, Miss Ryan has taken an active part in charity causes, aiding such campaigns as the March of Dimes, American Heart Association, Community Chest, and Medicare Alert, and performing for veterans in hospitals across the country."

Hillbillies on Parade

In the show's heyday, CBS marketing executives decided Hillbilly merchandise was a safe investment. "Yer dirn tootin'," Granny might say. CBS planned a $500,000 merchandising campaign during the sixties that exploited the characters with every type of toy, game, and sellable item imaginable.

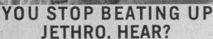

Bubblegum cards.

I DON'T CARE IF IT IS YOUR JOB, JUST TOUCH OUR GARBAGE & I'LL SHOOT.

JETHRO, YOU'RE GOING TO GET IN TROUBLE BATHING IN THE PARK FOUNTAIN.

Merchandisers produced two Clampett cars, complete with character figurines that sat in the seat and a model kit of the truck that could convert to Jethro's hot rod.

In addition, the Beverly Hillbillies' faces were splattered on bubblegum cards, comic books, a coloring book, jigsaw puzzles, T-shirts, and board games. Moreover, the craze for Elly May spawned a doll in her likeness, rope-tied jeans, and leggy paper doll cutouts. If the public was a-buyin', CBS was a-sellin'!

If you're looking for the theme song "The Ballad of Jed Clampett," it was recorded three times: First as a single by Jerry Scoggins (who sang the show's theme); Buddy Ebsen sang

YOU STOP BEATING UP JETHRO, HEAR?

THE LETTER WOULD MAKE MORE SENSE IF YOU COULD READ.

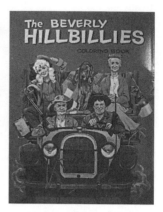

the theme on a 45 rpm; and later it was recorded by Lester Flatt and Earl Scruggs (who performed the instrumental for the show's opening).

Flatt & Scruggs' Greatest Hits (Columbia Records) includes "The Ballad of Jed Clampett" and the song "Pearl, Pearl, Pearl," which they performed on the show.

Television's Greatest Hits (by TeeVee Toons) includes a Flatt and Scruggs' version of "The Ballad of Jed Clampett," available on stereo LP and compact disc.

Other items for sale included:

- The Beverly Hillbillies lunchbox and thermos (Aladin of Knoxville, Tennessee).
- Granny and Jed Halloween costume and mask (Ben Cooper and Halco).
- Whitman hardback storybook, *The Saga of Wildcat Creek.*
- View Master reels (by GAF).
- Kellogg's Corn Flakes offered to kids a Beverly Hillbillies Bubble Pipe for twenty-five cents with one box top. The "corncob pipe" needed no soap—only water. "Shore is a heap o' fun!" the cereal box advertised.
- Sheet music published for "The Ballad of Jed Clampett" (Carolintone Music).
- A *Beverly Hillbillies* stereo LP (Harmony label, Columbia Records) sung by the cast with such "memorable" favorites as "A Long Talk with That Boy," sung by Jed

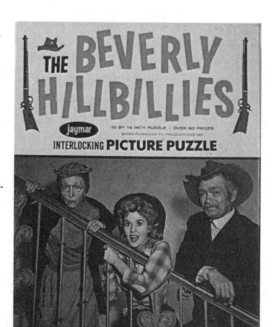

The Beverly Hillbillies

and Jethro; the cast's rendition of "Jethro's a Powerful Man"; and "Love of Money," warbled by Drysdale and Miss Jane.

- "Granny's Mini-Skirt," a 45 rpm recording (Nashwood Records). The flip side was "Bring on the Show." Both were sung by Irene Ryan, with vocal backgrounds by the Markleys.
- Buddy Ebsen sings: a 45 rpm of Ebsen singing "Mail Order Bride" and "The Ballad of Jed Clampett" (MGM Records).
- The Beverly Hillbillies Game (average-size board game, by Standard Toycraft).
- Tru-Vue Magic Eyes story set (by GAF).
- Beverly Hillbillies Picture Puzzle (Jaymar company produced sixteen interlocking jigsaw and frame-tray puzzles).
- Beverly Hillbillies Punch-Out Book (Whitman).
- Beverly Hillbillies coloring books (Whitman, Golden Books).
- Beverly Hillbillies "Set Back" card game (Milton Bradley).
- Beverly Hillbillies Cartoon Kit (Coloforms released two different versions).
- *The Clampetts of Beverly Hills* and *The Beverly Hillbillies Live It Up* (Avon pocket paperbacks).
- Elly May Cut-Out Doll Book (Watkins-Strathmore Company).
- Clampett Family songbooks (Alfred Music Company issued arrangements of the show's music for accordion, guitar, piano/organ, and clarinet).
- "Hillbillies Hats" (Tandy Leather Company).
- Beverly Hillbillies Television Truck (Model kit designed by George Barris, produced by Craft Masters).
- Black felt Hillbillies hat (Arlington Hat Company).
- Beverly Hillbillies Plastic Palette Coloring Set (Standard Toycraft).
- Beverly Hillbillies Sliding Puzzle (commonly known as a "palm puzzle," released by Roalex).
- Beverly Hillbillies comic books (Dell, series of twenty-one).
- Bubblegum cards (Fleer produced sixty-six cards).
- Elly May dolls (Kellogg's premium).

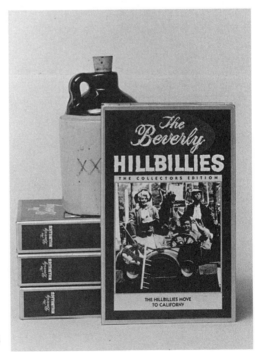

Remastered from the original negatives are pristine-quality prints on videotape, available from Columbia House Video Library. *Courtesy of Columbia House*

Hillbillies on Parade (continued)

- Beverly Hillbillies large plastic truck (Ideal). Includes plastic character figures in the seats. The truck winds up by a crank in front and moves. This is the most sought after and the most expensive of the show's collected merchandise.
- *The Saturday Evening Post* (February 2, 1963, featuring the four main cast members on the cover, was photographed by Allan Grant. The portrait was inspired by the famous *American Gothic* image painted by Grant Wood).

The Hillbillies are available on affordable home video through CBS/Fox. *Courtesy of CBS/Fox Video*

7

"...Movie Stars..."

In the age of recycling, "The Beverly Hillbillies" is a frontrunner in what may become a bombardment of television shows being re-created for the motion picture screen.

Star Trek did it with phenomenal success. *The Addams Family* film—an intended divorce from the original TV show—started a trend, because studios have begun dusting off other sitcoms like "F-Troop," "Gilligan's Island," "The Brady Bunch," "The Flintstones," and "Bewitched." Some say translating a TV show into a motion picture is a perfectly natural progression. Others say its a lazy way out since more than ever, fresh ideas for comedy in motion pictures are slow to arrive.

Paul Henning isn't worried. He is mildly disappointed, however, that the opening shot of the new $25 million motion picture on his famous Hillbillies is *not* going to be a nude scene of Elly May, like originally written in the screenplay by Larry Konner & Mark Rosenthal and Alex Herschlag. "That would have been an eye-opener," Henning says, laughing. "Afterall, Elly May is supposed to be a beautiful young woman."

Henning "leased" his Hillbilly characters to producer David Permut, who was responsible for the film version of *Dragnet*, star-

The newfangled Beverly Hillbillies. *Photograph by Bonnie Schiffman; Twentieth Century Fox*

ring Dan Aykroyd and Tom Hanks. It has taken more than five years, but finally, in cinematic splendor, Jed and all his kin will stike oil and move to Beverly. Hills that is. Movie stars. Box office gold.

And if it doesn't pan out with movie audiences?

"I'm not worried about that," Henning says. "My work is on film, on television . . . I don't think anything will disturb the original show—good or bad. I wish them a lot of luck. I hope the picture is great, because the possibilities are there."

In essence, the new Twentieth Century Fox TV-retread of "The Beverly Hillbillies" expands Henning's original pilot episode that

The Beverly Hillbillies

laid the tracks for the whole journey to Californy. Director Penelope Spheeris, who choreographed another great clashing of cultures in the sleeper hit *Wayne's World*, says "The Beverly Hillbillies" is one of her all-time favorite TV shows. She knows she holds a national treasure in her hand. That's why her choice of Cloris Leachman for Granny was not second-guessed.

Leachman *wanted* the role of Granny. When the actress came in to read for the role already dressed in a gray wig, a hat, Granny glasses, and a prairie-dress, Spheeris flipped. "How can you go wrong?" said the director.

In some shots, Cloris Leachman resembled Irene Ryan's Granny so much it was eerie.

Photograph by Steve Cox

Leachman, a finalist in the 1946 Miss America pageant, studied acting with New York's respected Actor's Studio in the 1950s. Her subsequent film and television credits didn't dampen Spheeris's enthusiasm to hire her, either. Leachman won an Acadamy Award for Best Supporting Actress as the lonely Ruth Popper in *The Last Picture Show*. Perhaps she's best remembered by television audiences as the quirky Phyllis Lindstrom on "The Mary Tyler Moore Show," a role that earned her two Emmy Awards during the seventies.

In a mansion where Paul Henning visited filming, the man who created the role looked at Cloris Leachman dressed as Granny and closely observed her wistful movements—all reminiscent of Irene Ryan, he noted. He nodded his head and smiled.

"She's damned good," was all he said.

Jim Varney was a boy from the south end of Lexington, Kentucky, when "The Beverly Hillbillies" premiered on television airwaves after endless weeks of hype and anticipation. He clearly recalls the fall evening in 1962, because his family had just made the invest-

Paul Henning and his wife, Ruth, visit with Cloris Leachman on the set of the new film version of *The Beverly Hillbillies*. Photograph by Steve Cox

The Beverly Hillbillies

ment of a black and white television console, and everyone was gathered around to watch this new show.

"I remember my mother said she really wanted to see this new program about hillbillies, 'cause she's a hillbilly," Varney says. "The show was hilarious . . . all the cliché hillbilly things were in there . . . things we were all familiar with."

Now, a smidgen past thirty years have gone by, and this time around Jed Clampett is played by actor Jim Varney. In addition to Varney and Leachman, the film also stars Lily Tomlin as Jane Hathaway, Dabney Coleman as Milburn Drysdale, Erika Eleniak as Elly May, and Diedrich Bader as Jethro.

The wide-screen adaptation of Paul Henning's characters takes us back to the hills to reveal a bit more about the day Jed Clampett struck oil, the trip out West, and a few winding roads in between. The characterizations are very much the same, and misconceptions have been updated: Elly May turns a satellite dish into a bird bath; when someone in a vehicle flips off the Clam-

Erika Eleniak plays the new Elly May, complete with critters. *Photograph by Deana Newcomb; Twentieth Century Fox*

petts in Los Angeles traffic, they think it's a friendly gesture and happily return the middle finger.

Although many actors were considered to play Jed Clampett (Tom Skerritt, Steve Martin, Sam Elliot, Dennis Weaver, Jason Robards, Ben Johnson, Jack Warden among them), Jim Varney playing the head of the Clampett clan may just be a natural. He knows his mountain folk.

"There are hillbillies in the Ozarks and hillbillies in the Appalachian Mountains," Varney explains. "The Tennessee branch of hillbillies around the Smoky Mountains are called 'ridge-runners,' an' when you get to Georgia, they call 'em 'crackers' or 'rednecks.'

"Y' know where the word 'redneck' came from?" he asks, using his cigarette as a beat. "From the old plow men. They wore a cap, but the sun beat down on them all day and their necks became red from leaning over the plow. So, basically, a poor itinerant farmer would be a redneck."

Varney was born forty-some years ago with hillbilly blood running through his veins, and now he's about to become one of the nation's most famous mountaineers, although a bit shorter and younger than the original Jed. He has never met Buddy Ebsen, he says, although he'd like to and there seems to be a tinge of uneasiness about the boondockers he has to fill.

"I was definitely influenced by Buddy Ebsen," Varney admits. "Our director, Penelope Spheeris, kept stressing the calmness and cool nature of the character. Like hillbilly Zen. At peace with the world, even though Jed had never been outside his holler."

For the past eleven years, Varney has slicked back his hair, put on a cap, and stuck his mug right up into the cameras for a series of "Ernest" motion pictures (*Ernest Goes to Camp*, *Ernest Saves Christmas*) and heavily run commercials ("Hey Vern!"). As Jed, it was difficult for Varney to suppress so much of the broad comedy he's employed as Ernest. "They had to hold me down a little bit," he says.

This is really the first "breakaway" role that Varney has been handed. It may surprise you to know he began as a Shakespearean-trained actor with an apprenticeship from the nationally acclaimed Barter Theatre in Virginia. "Not in my wildest dreams did I think I'd play Jed Clampett in a movie," he says. "Not in my wildest dreams did I think Ernest would become such a mainstay in my career."

For Varney, fighting the image of Ernest P. Worrell—the rubber-faced hick who made him famous—is merely half of the battle here. Delicately adjusting audiences' fixation with the original "Beverly Hillbillies" sitcom is going to be something else, he says.

Lily Tomlin seriously hesitated before accepting the role of Jane Hathaway for that very reason. "That's the kind of thing that hits you," she says. "How can you possibly win at this? So many people are such fans of the Hillbillies and know the show inside out.

"At first I felt like it might be treacherous," Tomlin says. "Then it felt like it was correct. I felt like I was given permission from the

Miss Hathaway (Lily Tomlin) attempts to locate Granny by hiring a private investigator—Barnaby Jones.
Photograph by Deana Newcomb; Twentieth Century Fox

Zeitgeist or something. It felt fine. This movie is a homage to the original cast. It's been done with a light hand and it's great fun."

During the sixties, when "The Beverly Hillbillies" first aired, Lily Tomlin was out doing club dates and struggling to make it as a comedienne in a predominantly male career. This was before she landed "Laugh-In," and Ernestine, the irreverent telephone operator. "I was totally acquainted with the 'Hillbillies,' but I didn't watch the show that much back then because I was out on the road trying to make it," she says.

Her path never crossed that of the late Nancy Kulp—TV's Miss Jane—although Tomlin did her homework, studied videotapes of the series, and tuned in as much as she could to reruns. "There's certainly some of Nancy Kulp in my Jane Hathaway, even if I'm wearing light hair," she says. "We *wanted* it to be reminiscent."

Tomlin prefaces: the magnitude of Miss Jane's passion has escalated, but not the target. "In this," she points out, "Jane Hathaway is much more aggressive and confident. She may as well be brought up on sexual harassment charges."

In his film debut, twenty-six-year-old actor Diedrich Bader plays 6'2" Jethro with tossled hair, a big grin, and a hearty appetite. Bader had done Shakespeare and episodic television before he landed the meaty role of "cultural icon," Jethro Bodine.

The shock didn't really hit him until a few days after the grueling four-month shooting schedule had ended.

"I was having a few beers with a friend and I just stopped for a second and went, 'Wait a minute! I just played Jethro Bodine!' " he says.

Bader is an unadulterated fan of the TV show and can tell you anything you may want to know about a man named Jed. "I have watched the show since I was a kid. It was very much a part of my childhood," Bader says, adding that he "totally identified" with Jethro. "I was the youngest kid. Always the goofball. To me, Jethro was the funniest on the show."

Bader admits to toiling over the role and questioning his every move. "If I did a direct imitation of Max Baer as Jethro, that

Diedrich Bader as Jethro. *Photograph by Deana Newcomb; Twentieth Century Fox*

would take me through about five minutes into the movie. O.K., then what?"

Bader decided to do it his way and borrow a little from Max Baer. "What I tried to do was something different," he says. "It still had to be recognizable, like going back to the old neighborhood. I'm not re-creating the role, just assuming the character. It's not necessarily the same exact character, either. Kind of nebulous. Some of the character traits such as the high-gear enthusiasm and the constant smiling I got from Max Baer on the show."

The real test of Bader's thespian muscles was his brief appearance as Jethrine Bodine, Jethro's homely sister who flies out on a plane with a hundred other hillbillies to visit the Clampetts in Californy.

Bader pulled up his jean pantleg. "See, the hair's growing back." During the seven days it took to shoot the Jethrine scene, Bader shaved his face and legs twice a day and required massive amounts of pancake makeup to get the right look for Jethrine.

Double Bodine: Diedrich Bader, who plays Jethro in the new film version, meets the original Jethro, Max Baer, Jr. *Photograph by Steve Cox*

Bader's Jethrine is "very feminine," he says, versus Max Baer's mock transvestite version of Jethrine in the television show. "I wanted to go all the way with it," Bader explains. "Jethrine on TV wore sleeveless dresses and you could plainly see Max Baer's muscles. At first, the wardrobe people wanted to put me in short sleeves also, but I wanted long sleeves. Otherwise, you might as well have me in a beard and smoking a cigar.

"There's a little bit of Marilyn Monroe and Vivien Leigh in Jethrine. And maybe a little bit of Blanche Dubois and Scarlett O'Hara in there, if you can imagine."

The Beverly Hillbillies

Study-up Now

- Like that of the TV show, the mansion seen in the film is *not* in Beverly Hills. A mansion in Los Angeles and one in Pasadena, California, served as the interior and exterior of the Clampett domain for this film.
- The truck seen in this film is nearly an exact duplicate of the original 1921 Oldsmobile four-cylinder used in the TV show. Custom auto expert George Barris (designer of the original Batmobile and the "Munsters" autos, etc.) supplied the replica for the film. The one and only original Hillbillies truck is now on permanent display at the Ralph Foster Museum on the campus of the School of the Ozarks in Branson, Missouri.
- Actor Robert Easton, sporting long blond hair and a lengthy light beard, can be spotted in the film's airplane scene. Known as the "Henry Higgins of Hollywood," Easton instructed the backwoods dialect to many of the movie's cast members. Ironically, Easton appeared in an episode of the Hillbillies TV series titled "Luke's Boy," where he played hick Beauregard Short, a suitor for Elly.
- Dolly Parton makes a cameo appearance in the film singing "Happy Birthday" at Jed's surprise party. On the set she was reunited with Lily Tomlin and Dabney Coleman, all costars from the motion picture *9 to 5*. Says Lily Tomlin: "We were going to try and add a line about it, like having Dolly ask Jane Hathaway, 'How's it goin' Miss Jane?' and I would say, 'Oh, just working nine to five.' We decided it really didn't fit, but it would've been funny."

Photograph by Gabi Rona

Episode Guide

Cast

Jed Clampett	Buddy Ebsen
Granny (Daisy Moses)	Irene Ryan
Elly May Clampett	Donna Douglas
Jethro Bodine	Max Baer, Jr.
Miss Jane Hathaway	Nancy Kulp
Milburn Drysdale	Raymond Bailey
Margaret Drysdale	Harriet MacGibbon
Pearl Bodine	Bea Benaderet

First Prime-time Telecast: September 26, 1962
Last Prime-time Telecast: September 7, 1971

The following is a complete list of every episode (106 in black and white, 168 in color). Episodes are in order of their airing, by title. GC: Guest Cast.

1. The Hillbillies of Beverly Hills (Pilot)

Jed Clampett sells his swamp full of oil to the O.K. Oil Company for $25 million and moves the family to Beverly Hills to live in a 35-room man-

---

Beverly habilliments: everything from their duds to
their dialogue was pure, authentic hillbilly.
Courtesy of Personality Photos, Inc.

sion. GC: Bea Benaderet (Cousin Pearl), Frank Wilcox (Mr. Brewster),
Bob Osborne (Jeffrey Taylor), Ron Hagerthy (Geologist).

2. Getting Settled
When they arrive at their mansion, wealthy Jed Clampett and his family
are mistaken by Miss Hathaway for a staff of insubordinate, backwoods
servants.

3. Meanwhile, Back at the Cabin
The Clampetts find that the luxuries of their new mansion are a poor
substitute for the comforts of their former mountain shack. GC: Bea
Benaderet (Pearl Bodine), Frank Wilcox (Mr. Brewster), Max Baer, Jr.
(Jethrine Bodine), Linda Kaye Henning (Voice of Jethrine).

4. The Clampetts Meet Mrs. Drysdale
When Mr. Drysdale describes his wife as a hypochondriac, the Clampetts
assume she must be a drunk.

The Beverly Hillbillies

5. Jed Buys Stock

When Drysdale advises the Clampetts to invest in stock, Jed rushes out to buy some cows, pigs, goats, and chickens—livestock! GC: Arthur Gould Porter (Ravenswood, the butler), Sirry Steffen (Marie, the maid).

6. Trick or Treat

The homesick Clampetts, unaware that it's Halloween night, decide to go calling on their Beverly Hills neighbors. GC: Bea Benaderet (Pearl), Phil Gordon (Jasper "Jazzbo" Depew), Teddy Eccles (Little boy), Frank Wilcox (Mr. Brewster), Max Baer, Jr. (Jethrine Bodine), Linda Kaye Henning (Voice of Jethrine), Shirley Mitchell (Governess).

7. The Servants

Milburn Drysdale attempts another step in the social renovation of the Clampetts by lending them his servants. GC: Arthur Gould Porter (Ravenswood), Sirry Steffen (Marie).

8. Jethro Goes to School

Jed enrolls Jethro in the Millicent Schuyler-Potts private school. Mrs. Potts, a teacher, is surprised to find out her new student is Jethro. GC:

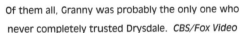

Of them all, Granny was probably the only one who never completely trusted Drysdale. *CBS/Fox Video*

Sonny Drysdale (Louis Nye) gives Elly a lesson in posture while attempting to transform her into a gracious lady. *Courtesy of Louis Nye*

The Beverly Hillbillies

Bea Benaderet (Pearl), Eleanor Audley (Mrs. Potts), Phil Gordon (Jasper Depew), Frank Wilcox (Mr. Brewster), Lisa Davis (Diane).

9. Elly's First Date

Elly May's first date with Mr. Drysdale's grown stepson, Sonny, ends in confusion before it even starts. GC: Louis Nye (Sonny Drysdale).

10. Pygmalion and Elly

Debonair Sonny Drysdale plays Pygmalion and Julius Caesar as he resumes his tempestuous courtship of Elly May. GC: Louis Nye (Sonny Drysdale).

11. Elly Races Jethrine

The Clampetts try to get Sonny to propose to Elly May before Cousin Pearl can get her hulky daughter Jethrine married to "Jazzbo" Depew. GC: Bea Benaderet (Pearl), Louis Nye (Sonny Drysdale), Phil Gordon (Jasper Depew), Max Baer, Jr. (Jethrine Bodine), Linda Kaye Henning (Voice of Jethrine).

12. The Great Feud

The Clampetts load up their shootin' irons for a march on the Drysdale estate after Sonny Drysdale jilts Elly May. GC: Sirry Steffen (Marie), Arthur Gould Porter (Ravenswood), Ken Drake (1st Psychiatrist), Lyle Talbot (2nd Psychiatrist).

13. Home for Christmas

The Clampetts take their first airplane ride to return to their mountain cabin for a surprise visit with Cousin Pearl. GC: Bea Benaderet (Pearl), Paul Winchell (Grandpa Winch), Frank Wilcox (Mr. Brewster), Jeanne Vaughn (1st Airline stewardess), Eilene Janssen (2nd Airline stewardess).

14. No Place Like Home

The Clampetts, home for the holidays, help Cousin Pearl attract Mr. Brewster, the oil company executive. GC: Bea Benaderet (Pearl), Paul Winchell (Homer Winch), Frank Wilcox (Mr. Brewster).

15. Jed Rescues Pearl

Pearl's efforts to snag the elusive Mr. Brewster seem doomed until he makes a ridiculous marriage proposal in public. GC: Bea Benaderet (Pearl), Elvia Allman (Elverna Bradshaw), Frank Wilcox (Mr. Brewster).

16. Back to Californy

Jed is confronted with too many cooks and not enough vittles when he invites Cousin Pearl and Jethrine to his Beverly Hills home. GC: Bea Benaderet (Pearl), Phil Gordon (Jasper Depew), Frank Wilcox (Mr. Brewster), Gloria Marshall (Airline stewardess), Max Baer, Jr. (Jethrine Bodine), Linda Kaye Henning (Voice of Jethrine).

17. Jed's Dilemma

Trying to cool down a feud between Granny and Pearl, Jed takes his family on a sightseeing tour of Beverly Hills. GC: Bea Benaderet (Pearl).

18. Jed Saves Drysdale's Marriage

Mr. Drysdale's marriage is threatened when he looks to the Clampetts for a housekeeper while his wife visits a health farm. GC: Bea Benaderet (Pearl).

19. Elly's Animals

Policemen and Elly May's animal friends converge on the Clampett estate when Cousin Pearl starts giving lessons in yodeling. GC: Bea

A police officer (Brian Kelly) dispatched to the Clampetts to investigate some smoke (Granny's still), becomes instantly infatuated with Elly May. *Viacom*

Benaderet (Pearl), Eddie Dean (1st Policeman), Peter Leeds (Joe), Brian Kelly (2nd Policeman), Karl Lukas (Frank). *Note:* Yodeling by singer Lucille Starr.

20. Jed Throws a Wingding

Two of Cousin Pearl's former suitors, Lester Flatt and Earl Scruggs, come to visit her in Beverly Hills. GC: Bea Benaderet (Pearl), Earl Scruggs (Himself), Lester Flatt (Himself), Midge Ware (Louise Scruggs), Joi Lansing (Gladys Flatt).

21. Jed Plays Solomon

Granny's campaign to halt Pearl's yodeling backfires when Granny calls the law and the police find Granny's still. GC: Bea Benaderet (Pearl), Eddie Dean (Sgt. Dean), Brian Kelly (Officer Kelly), Lucille Starr (Yodeler).

22. Duke Steals a Wife

Duke, Jed's trusty bloodhound, becomes a matchmaker for his master and Mademoiselle Denise, a glamorous Frenchwoman. GC: Bea Benaderet (Pearl), Narda Onyx (Mlle. Denise).

23. Jed Buys the Freeway

Con man Harry Jones tries to sell Jed the Hollywood Bowl, Griffith Park, and the Hollywood Freeway. GC: Bea Benaderet (Pearl), Jesse White (H. H. H. Jones), Dick O'Shea (Auto salesman).

24. Jed Becomes a Banker

Jed Clampett is made a bank vice president so he can compete in an interbank skeet tournament with partnerless Mr. Drysdale. GC: Charles Lane (Mr. Hacker), Lester Matthews (Mr. Pendleton), Jack Boyle (Photographer), Laura Shelton (Secretary).

25. The Family Tree

An authority on early American history finds evidence that Jed Clampett's ancestors preceded the *Mayflower* to America. GC: Bea Benaderet (Pearl), Rosemary DeCamp (Mrs. Standish).

26. Jed Cuts the Family Tree

Cousin Pearl gets a glamour treatment and tries to groom the Clampetts for their new status in high society. GC: Bea Benaderet (Pearl), Rosemary DeCamp (Mrs. Standish).

27. Granny's Spring Tonic

Jed takes a double dose of Granny's spring tonic and winds up in Lovers' Lane with a gold-digging bank secretary. GC: Bea Benaderet (Pearl), Lola Albright (Gloria Buckles). *Note:* Gloria Buckles was actually the name of Paul Henning's secretary.

28. Jed Pays His Income Tax

An IRS agent calls on the Clampetts and gets a roaring shotgun welcome from Granny. GC: Bea Benaderet (Pearl), Frank Wilcox (Mr. Brewster), John Stephenson (Mr. Landman), Ron Hagerthy (Geologist). *Note:* This episode includes flashback footage from the pilot.

29. The Clampetts and the Dodgers

While golfing, Los Angeles Dodgers coach Leo Durocher can't believe his eyes when he sees Jethro throw a baseball with such speed and accuracy. GC: Leo Durocher (Himself), Wally Cassell (Buzzie Bavasi), Skip Ward (Walsh Wesson), Norman Leavitt (Attendant), Jimmy Gaines (Little boy).

30. Duke Becomes a Father

Love returns for Jed when the glamorous Mlle. Denise returns from Paris to herald the arrival of a new litter of puppies. GC: Narda Onyx (Mlle. Denise).

31. The Clampetts Entertain

The board chairman of the Commerce Bank of Beverly Hills is determined to meet the bank's "ace financial wizard" and largest depositor—tycoon Jed Clampett. GC: Jim Backus (Marty van Ransohoff). *Note:* Marty Van Ransohoff was the chairman of the board for Filmways Television, the show's owners.

32. The Clampetts in Court

Jed acts as his own attorney when he's sued by an unscrupulous couple seeking $100,000 in damages for a fictitious automobile accident. GC:

Kathleen Freeman (Mabel Johnson), Murvyn Vye (James Johnson), Roy Roberts (Judge), Dean Harens (Attorney), Jess Kirkpatrick (Bailiff).

33. The Clampetts Get Psychoanalyzed

When Jethro requires a physical for school, he mistakenly goes to a psychiatrist who is befuddled by him. GC: Bea Benaderet (Pearl), Herbert Rudley (Dr. Twombly), Dick Wesson (Patient), Karen Norris (Nurse). Note: Twombly was actually actress Bea Benaderet's last name by marriage.

34. The Psychiatrist Gets Clampetted

A Beverly Hills psychiatrist pursues Granny instead of Pearl when Granny's secret love charm misfires. GC: Bea Benaderet (Pearl), Herbert Rudley (Dr. Twombly).

35. Elly Becomes a Secretary

Jed Clampett takes over Milburn Drysdale's job for one afternoon and wins the title "Banker of the Year" for him. GC: John Ashley (Bob Billington), Willis Bouchey (Mr. Willis), Patty Jo Harmon (Kitty), Bill Baldwin (Convention speaker).

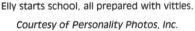

Elly starts school, all prepared with vittles.

Courtesy of Personality Photos, Inc.

36. Jethro's Friend

The Clampetts take a pampered eleven-year-old rich boy in to show him how to really enjoy himself. GC: Hayden Rorke (Wilkins), Michel Petit (Armstrong Dueser McHugh III) Note: Armstrong, Dueser & McHugh was the name of the public relations firm that handled some of the cast.

37. Jed Gets the Misery

To humor Granny, Jed fakes illness so that she can resume the doctoring practice that brought her fame in the hills. GC: Fred Clark (Dr. Clyburn).

38. Hair-Raising Holiday

Granny defies medical opposition to her own brand of mountain medicine as she reveals an astonishing ability to grow hair. GC: Fred Clark (Dr. Clyburn).

39. Granny's Garden

Her neighbors are aghast when Granny decides to start a vegetable garden on the grounds of the Clampett mansion.

40. Elly Starts to School

Elly May sparks a new trend in understated fashion when she enrolls at a finishing school for pampered rich girls. GC: Doris Packer (Mrs. Fenwick), Sharon Tate (Sharon), Joanna Barnes (Cynthia Fenwick), Tom Cound (Beasley).

41. The Clampett Look

Dressed as backwoods hillbillies, Cynthia Fenwick and her mother call on the Clampetts, thinking they are the new avante-garde socialites. GC: Doris Packer (Mrs. Fenwick), Joanna Barnes (Cynthia Fenwick).

42. Jethro's First Love

Jethro, after a man-to-man talk with Jed, wastes no time in finding a brassy, burlesque dancer for a girlfriend. GC: Barbara Nichols (Chickadee Laverne), Sharon Tate (Janet Trego).

43. Chickadee Returns

Jethro decides he wants to get married, so he chooses Chickadee Laverne, not knowing she's a brassy burlesque dancer. GC: Barbara Nichols (Chickadee), Sharon Tate (Janet Trego).

No modern showers for these Hillbillies! *Viacom*

44. The Clampetts Are Overdrawn

Jed Clampett receives the startling news that his multimillion-dollar account is overdrawn by $34.70 because the bank mixed up the statements with another Clampett. GC: King Donovan (Jake "J.D." Clam-

Penniless actor Jake Clampett (King Donovan) attempts to bilk Jed out of his fortune when he realizes they have the same last name.

Courtesy of Filmways

pett), Shirley Mitchell (Opal Clampett), Sharon Tate (Janet Trego), Gil Perkins (Pool man), Robert Foulk (Policeman), Jack Boyle (Photographer), Dick Crockett (Paving man).

45. The Clampetts Go Hollywood
Under the noxious influence of imposter Jake Clampett, the Clampetts turn Hollywood. GC: King Donovan (Jake Clampett), Shirley Mitchell (Opal Clampett), Sharon Tate (Janet Trego).

46. Turkey Day
Plans for a holiday feast at the Clampett mansion go awry when Elly May makes a pet of the dinner. GC: Benny Rubin (1st Indian), George Sawaya (2nd Indian).

47. The Garden Party
Mrs. Drysdale gives a lavish garden party and loses her guests to the lively Clampetts next door. GC: Arthur Gould Porter (Ravenswood), Curt Massey (Violinist), Murray Pollock (Young man), Sharon Tate (Young girl). *Note:* Curt Massey, who plays a violinist, composed the background music for the show.

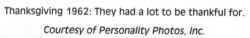

Thanksgiving 1962: They had a lot to be thankful for.

Courtesy of Personality Photos, Inc.

The Beverly Hillbillies

48. Elly Needs a Maw

Jed decides that his tomboy daughter, Elly (who has taken up motorcycle riding), needs a mother to make her a lady. GC: Doris Packer (Mrs. Fenwick), Sharon Tate (Janet Trego), Tom Cound (Beasley).

49. The Clampetts Get Culture

The Clampetts try unsuccessfully to participate in some of the more civilized pleasures of Beverly Hills. GC: Eleanor Audley (Mrs. Potts), Sharon Tate (Janet Trego), Don Orlando (Italian tailor).

CBS/Fox Video

50. Christmas at the Clampetts

Christmas Day finds the Clampetts confused by their expensive gifts, all from Mr. Drysdale. GC: Arthur Gould Porter (Ravenswood).

51. A Man for Elly

Quirt Manly, celebrated star of TV westerns, is invited to the Clampett mansion to try to tame Elly May. GC: Henry Gibson (Quirt Manly), Amedee Chabot (Girl).

52. The Giant Jackrabbit

Aired January 8, 1964

Written by Paul Henning and Mark Tuttle

Directed by Richard Whorf

An Australian banker sends Drysdale a live kangaroo as a joke and Granny thinks she has discovered a five-foot jackrabbit. When no one can find the varmit, Jed assumes Granny's been hittin' the jug. GC: Arthur Gould Porter (Ravenswood), Sharon Tate (Janet Trego), Peter Bourne (Bill Tinsman), Kathy Kersh (Marian Billington).

Note: No one quite knows why, but this particular episode grabbed an unbelievable 65 share and a 44.0 rating. To date, it remains the highest-rated half-hour television program since 1960, when Nielsen established its current rating system.

Granny has hasenpfeffer in mind. *CBS/Fox Video*

53. The Girl from Home

A young beauty contest winner from back home and her father come to visit Jethro with marriage on their minds. GC: Muriel Landers (Essiebelle), Peter Whitney (Lafe Crick), Chet Stratton (Jewelry salesman), Kathy Kersh (Marian Billington).

54. Lafe Lingers On

Backwoods freeloader Lafe Crick, in search of money, lingers at the Clampett mansion as an unwanted guest. GC: Peter Whitney (Lafe Crick).

55. The Race for Queen

Elly May enters—and almost wins—the Miss Beverly Hills beauty contest. GC: Bob Cummings (Himself), Susan Hart (Candy Davis), Kathy Kersh (Marian Billington), John Alvin (Photographer).

56. The Critter Doctor

Granny gets her dander up when she confuses an insecticide salesman with the "critter doctor" Elly May has called. GC: Mark Goddard (Jim Gardner), Russell Collins (Dr. Martin).

57. Lafe Returns

Still trying to get his hands on the Clampett loot, Lafe Crick returns, ostensibly to give Granny a pawpaw tree. GC: Peter Whitney (Lafe Crick), Bobs Watson (Fred Penrod).

58. Son of Lafe Returns

Lafe Crick brings his hillbilly son, Dub, to Beverly Hills to court Elly May. GC: Peter Whitney (Lafe Crick), Conlan Carter (Dub Crick), Bobs Watson (Fred Penrod).

59. The Clampetts Go Fishing

The Clampetts embark on an unusual fishing trip at the famed Marineland of the Pacific. GC: Mark Tapscott (Marine sergeant), Glen Stensel (Air Force lieutenant).

60. A Bride for Jed

Jane Hathaway comes up with a unique idea on how to find a wife for Jed Clampett, with disastrous results. GC: Earl Scruggs (Himself), Midge Ware (Louise Scruggs), Joi Lansing (Gladys Flatt), Adele Clair (Contestant).

61. Granny vs. the Weather Bureau

Granny's infuriated when her old-fashioned ways of predicting the weather are pitted against the Weather Bureau's advanced technology. She uses Cecil, her weather beetle. GC: Quinn O'Hara (Weather girl), Helen Kleeb (Addison's secretary), John McGiver (Justin Addison).

62. Another Neighbor

Several of Beverly Hills' more prominent citizens are more than a little affected when they sample Granny's spring tonic. GC: Jean Willes (Countess Maria), Susan Hart (Candy Davis), Burt Mustin (Humphrey, the chauffeur).

63. The Bank Raising

Invited to the dignified ground-breaking for a new bank, the Clampetts confuse the event with an old-fashioned barn raisin'. GC: Lester Matthews (Mr. Pendleton), Bill Baldwin (Radio announcer), Addison Richards (Mr. Lucas), Kathy Kersh (Marian Billington).

64. The Great Crawdad Hunt

Two Beverly Hills financiers continue to probe the mysterious "crawdad" stock held by that inscrutable financial wizard, J. D. Clampett. GC: Peter Leeds (Harry Sledge), Addison Richards (Mr. Lucas), Lester Matthews (Mr. Pendleton).

65. The Dress Shop

On the advice of Mr. Drysdale, the Clampetts become the owners of "House of Renée," the most exclusive dress shop in Beverly Hills. They rename it "House of Granny." GC: Natalie Schafer (Madame Renée), Marjorie Bennett (Mrs. Langwell).

66. The House of Granny

The Clampetts' new exclusive dress shop opens before dawn and becomes "The House of Granny"—complete with cracker barrel and a potbellied stove. GC: Ray Kellogg (Policeman), Maurice Marsac (Doorman), George Cisar (Police sergeant), Edna Skinner (Mrs. Wright).

67. The Continental Touch

Snooty Mrs. Drysdale mistakes Elly May for a European princess and excitedly plans a lavish party in her honor. GC: Janine Grandel (Madame Potvin), Maurice Marsac (Maurice).

68. Jed, Incorporated

Jed does business in his own way when Drysdale forms Clampco, Inc., as a tax shelter for Jed.

69. Granny Learns to Drive

After a taxi ride, Granny thinks the driver is trying to get fresh with her. The cabdriver is so confused, he thinks the Clampett mansion is a private psychiatric hospital, the Hillbillies patients, and Drysdale their doctor. GC: Mel Blanc (Cabbie, Dick Burton), Harry Lauter (Motorcycle cop).

70. Cabin in Beverly Hills

Drysdale's remedy for Granny's homesickness starts a social revolution when a young girl thinks the Hillbillies are Drysdale's slaves living in a tiny cabin behind the mansion. GC: Sheila James (Ginny Jennings), John Stephenson (Professor Graham), Jack Bannon (Man).

71. Jed Foils a Home Wrecker

Jed and Drysdale foil Mrs. Drysdale's plan to tear down the makeshift cabin that was built for Granny on the Clampett estate. GC: Sheila James (Ginny Jennings), John Stephenson (Professor Graham), Mike Ross (Al Ledbetter).

72. Jethro's Graduation

When Jethro misses his sixth grade graduation ceremony, Skipper the chimp takes his place. GC: Eleanor Audley (Mrs. Potts), Mike Barton (Boy 1), Happy Derman (Boy 2), Lisa Davis (Diana), Donald Foster (Theodore Switzer).

73. Jed Becomes a Movie Mogul

Jed Clampett becomes a movie mogul after Drysdale acquires controlling stock in Mammoth Studios, a motion picture corporation, for him. GC: Sallie Janes (Miss Swenson), Milton Frome (Lawrence Chapman), Russ Conway (Director), John Abbott (Sir Trevor Gielgud Burton-Guiness), Alvy Moore (Alvin), Ray Kellogg (Gateman). Note: Incorporated in this episode is footage of Rock Hudson and Doris Day trimmed from their yet-to-be-released film *Send Me No Flowers*.

74. Clampett City

Overjoyed to discover a rustic village on the back lot of the Mammoth Studios, the Clampetts decide to settle there. GC: Milton Frome (Lawrence Chapman), Sallie Janes (Miss Swenson), Don Megowan (Monster), Elvia Allman (Actress), Phil Gordon (Actor), Herb Ellis, Sidney Clute, Kip King, and Ray Kellogg (as the Producers).

75. Clampett City General Store

The Clampetts take part in a movie epic produced at their studio. GC: Sallie Janes (Miss Swenson), Milton Frome (Larry Chapman), Theodore Marcuse (Nero), Nestor Paiva (Auctioneer).

76. Hedda Hopper's Hollywood

Famous newspaper columnist Hedda Hopper joins the battle against Drysdale's plan to destroy Mammoth Studios. GC: Hedda Hopper (Herself), Don Haggerty (1st Policeman), Bill Baldwin (Himself), Ted Fish (2nd Policeman).

Hedda Hopper stops in to meet motion picture mogul Jed Clampett, who is filming a silent movie at his Mammoth Studios. *Courtesy of Personality Photos, Inc.*

77. Doctor Jed Clampett

Granny is jealous when Jed receives an honorary "doctor's" degree from Greely College. GC: Cully Richards (Bus driver), Richard St. John (Dean Cromwell), Virginia Sale (Chicken woman), Fabian Dean (Knife thrower), Hazel Shermet (Mother), Tina Marie Brockert (Child), Roy Rogers (Fire-eater).

78. Jed the Heartbreaker

In another effort to drive the uncouth Clampetts from Beverly Hills, Mrs. Drysdale attempts a new tactic.

79. Back to Marineland

Anxious to serve in the military, Jethro heads for Marineland—to join the U.S. Marines. GC: Sharon Tate (Janet Trego), Robert Carson (Marineland manager).

80. Teenage Idol

Johnny Poke, singing idol of millions, is reunited with his old friends the Clampetts. GC: Jesse Pearson (Johnny Poke), Alan Reed (Eddie Colton), Susan Walther and Marie Elena (Teenagers).

81. The Widow Poke Arrives

In one of her periodic campaigns to get Jed married, Granny secretly summons an old and marriageable acquaintance. GC: Ellen Corby (Emma Poke), Jesse Pearson (Johnny Poke).

82. The Ballet

Mrs. Drysdale tries to enlist Jed Clampett's financial support for the struggling Beverly Hills Ballet Company. GC: Leon Belasco (Victor Gregory), Roy Fitzell, Barrie Duffus, Diane Reese, Kim Condon, Consuela Moran, and Lavra Lamb (Dancers).

83. The Boarder

Granny decides to convert the mansion into a boardinghouse, and the first boarder mistakenly turns out to be Mrs. Drysdale's militantly efficient English butler. GC: Arthur Treacher (Pinckney).

Gentleman's gentleman Arthur Treacher tries to mold the Hillbillies. *Viacom*

84. The Boarder Stays

Pinckney, the English butler, is engaged to instruct culture to the Clampetts. GC: Arthur Treacher (Pinckney).

85. Start the New Year Right

Learning that Mrs. Drysdale is in the hospital because of a nervous ailment, the sympathetic Hillbillies pay her a visit. GC: Sue England (1st Nurse), Les Tremayne (Dr. Stuyvesant), Jill Jarmyn (2nd Nurse).

86. Clampett General Hospital

Having "rescued" Mrs. Drysdale from the hospital, the Clampetts try their hands at curing her with nerve tonic. GC: Jean Howell (Nurse), Willis Bouchey (Dr. Sanders).

87. The Movie Starlet

Jethro falls desperately in love with Kitty Devine, a volatile young movie starlet, and desperately wants to marry her. When she finds out his uncle owns the studio, she latches onto him. GC: Sharon Farrell (Kitty Devine), William Newell (1st Gate guard), Bernie Kopell (Jerry Best), Rodney Bell (2nd Gate guard).

88. Elly in the Movies

Through a mix-up, film star Dash Riprock mistakes Jane Hathaway for his new leading lady, Elly May Clampett. GC: Larry Pennell (Dash), Bill Quinn (Tom Kelly), Sally Mills (1st Girl), Ann Henry (2nd Girl), Diane Bond (3rd Girl), Marilee Summers (4th Girl).

89. Dash Riprock, You Cad

Elly May loses her second movie star boyfriend to plain Jane, whose mysterious power over men continues to baffle the Clampetts. GC: Larry Pennell (Dash Riprock), Sharon Tate (Janet Trego), Jeff Davis (Biff Steel), Dermot A. Cronin (Crunch Hardtack), Kent Miller (Tab Strong), Jack Bannon (Bolt Upright), Glenn Wilder (Race Burley), Murray Alper (Studio driver).

90. Clampett À-Go-Go

The Clampetts care for a madcap artist who wrecks his car when he sees Elly May in a bathing suit. GC: Alan Reed, Jr. (Sheldon Epps), Larry Pennell (Dash Riprock).

91. Granny's Romance

Mr. Drysdale forces an elderly playboy who is on the bank's board of directors into courting Granny. GC: Sylvia Lewis (Phyllis), Kent Smith (Clifton Cavanaugh).

92. Jed's Temptation

Granny sets out to save Jed from the evils of gambling and winds up enjoying it herself. GC: Sylvia Lewis (Phyllis), Iris Adrian (Wife), Don Rickles (Fred), Ralph Montgomery (Usher).

93. Double Naught Jethro

Jethro gives up his ambition of becoming a brain surgeon to become the James Bond type and accepts an undercover assignment. GC: Sharon Tate (Janet Trego), Joyce Nizzari (Mabel Slocum), Roy Roberts (Cushing).

94. Clampett's Millions

A rival banker from Merchants Bank attempts to lure the Clampett millions from Milburn Drysdale's loving care. GC: Roy Roberts (John Cushing), Joyce Nizzari (Mabel Slocum).

95. Drysdale's Dog Days

Granny insists on seeing the $11 million that is her share of Jed's fortune and demands that Drysdale produce it in cash. GC: Grandon Rhodes (Judge), Steve Brodie (Guard), John Day (Chauffeur).

96. Brewster's Honeymoon

An oil company executive spends a strange honeymoon in a mountain cabin in Beverly Hills, courtesy of the Clampetts GC: Frank Wilcox (Mr. Brewster), Lisa Seagram (Edythe).

97. Flatt, Clampett, and Scruggs

Granny suffers from homesickness until two old friends, Lester Flatt and Earl Scruggs, arrive in Beverly Hills and put her in show business. GC: Lester Flatt (Himself), Earl Scruggs (Himself), Frank Scannell (Stage manager).

98. Jed and the Countess

Spring-tonic time brings the Countess von Holstein back for another intoxicating visit with the Clampetts. GC: Jean Willes (Countess Maria), Burt Mustin (Humphrey).

99. Big Daddy, Jed

Sheldon Epps, the extraordinary beatnik, pays a return visit to the Clampetts to borrow "bread" from Jed. GC: Marianne Gaba (Squirrel), Richard Lerner (Wiggy), Paul De Rolf (Horace), Alan Reed, Jr. (Sheldon Epps), Keva Page (Shaky).

100. Cool School Is Out

Granny turns beatnik when she visits the Parthenon West coffeehouse to rescue Elly May and Jethro from a band of beatniks. GC: Marianne Gaba (Squirrel), Richard Lerner (Wiggy), Paul De Rolf (Horace), Alan Reed, Jr. (Sheldon Epps), Keva Page (Shaky).

Groovy: Elly turns, like, cool beatnik. *Courtesy of Personality Photos, Inc.*

101. The Big Bank Battle

Jed Clampett is offered a bank vice presidency—an inducement to get him to transfer his millions to another bank. GC: Roy Roberts (John Cushing), Sue Casey (Roberta Grahman).

102. The Clampetts vs. Automation

When a computer replaces one of Drysdale's underpaid bookkeepers, the displaced worker finds real friends in the Clampetts. GC: Byron Foulger (Leroy Lester), Sharon Tate (Janet Trego).

103. Luke's Boy

Granny once again thinks she's got a guy for Elly. GC: Pat Winters (Ann Gardner), Chanin Hale (Linda Curry), Robert Easton (Beauregard Short), Edythe Williams (Girl).

104. The Brewsters Return

The Clampetts force crude (but well-intentioned) hospitality upon oil man John Brewster and his cultured bride. GC: Frank Wilcox (John Brewster), Hal Taggart (Walter McKeegan), Lisa Seagram (Edythe).

105. Jed, the Bachelor

Granny finally makes good her threat to go home to the hills. She takes to the road and winds up in Las Vegas. GC: Peter Leeds (Truck driver), Julie Van Zandt (Policewoman), Ray Kellogg (Policeman), La Rue Farlow (Woman).

106. The Art Center

The Hillbillies produce a ghastly collection of "art" works for a new Beverly Hills art gallery. GC: Walter Woolf King (George Engel), Chet Stratton (Fredericks), Gay Gordon (Model).

107. Admiral Jed Clampett

Jed Clampett, wearing a vice admiral's uniform, mistakes a U.S. Navy destroyer for a yacht Drysdale wants him to buy. GC: David Frankham

"Admiral Jed Clampett" was the first episode filmed in color. *Courtesy of Buddy Ebsen*

The Beverly Hillbillies

(Naval lieutenant), Rick Cooper (Ensign), Mark Evans (Seaman), Frank Coghlin (Helmsman), Garrison True (Radarman), Ray Kellogg (Speedboat operator). Note: This is the premiere episode for the fourth season and the first shot in color.

108. That Old Black Magic

Granny is convinced that Mrs. Drysdale has used "black magic" to turn herself into a crow. GC: Dave Willock (Elevator starter), Tris Coffin (Psychiatrist), Allison McKay (Receptionist), John Gallaudet (Veterinarian).

109. The Sheik

A sheik from the Middle East makes Jed Clampett a present of four dancing girls and then falls for Elly May. GC: Dan Seymour (Sheik), Naji Gabbay (Aide), Charlotte Knight (Newshen), Frank Wilcox (Brewster), Bill Baldwin (Himself), Phil Gordon (Reporter), Nai Bonet, Diane Bond, Marianna Case, and Lisa Britton (Dancing girls).

Dan Seymour plays a sheik who talks to Granny about possible induction into his harem. *Viacom*

110. The Private Eye

Jethro (as Double-naught spy) winds up an unwitting accomplice in a plot to burglarize Drysdale's bank. GC: Donald Curtis (Barker), James Seay (Detective), Eileen O'Neill (Kay).

111. Possum Day

Drysdale desperately tries to arrange a Possum Day festival to keep the Clampetts from going back home. GC: Sharon Tate (Janet Trego), Jack Daly (Driver).

112. The Possum Parade

Drysdale continues his frantic efforts to promote a Possum Day parade for the Clampetts. GC: Barney Elmore (Chauffeur), Maurice Kelly (Man), Sharon Tate (Janet Trego), Bill Baldwin (Himself), Francisco Ortega (Man).

Vote for Granny! *Courtesy of Personality Photos, Inc.*

113. The Clampetts Play the Rams

Jethro discovers that it's his color TV and not him that the pretty maid next door likes. GC: Nina Shipman (Linda), Beecey Carlson (Cook).

114. The Courtship of Elly

Granny distills a love potion intended to land a husband for her "spinster" Elly May because the youngun is past fourteen. GC: Van Williams (Dean Peters).

115. A Real Nice Neighbor

Drysdale and Granny try to marry off Jed to a frumpy housemaid they have mistaken for a millionaire. GC: Kathleen Freeman (Agnes), William Bakewell (Chauffeur).

116. The Poor Farmer

The Clampetts think a dieting billionaire is a starving farmer, and they try to fatten him up. GC: Sebastion Cabot (Billionaire Lucas Sebastian), Lester Matthews (Fleming Pendleton), Hal Baylor (Joe), William Forrest (Canady).

117. Hoedown À-Go-Go

The senior Clampetts plan an old-fashioned barn dance, but Elly May and Jethro turn it into a rock 'n' roll blast. GC: Paul De Rolf (Specialty dancer), The Enemys (Themselves), The Garrett Dancers.

118. Mrs. Drysdale's Father

Mrs. Drysdale's father is a broke Bostonian who tries to get the Clampetts to gamble their fortune away. Jed is introduced to the game of pool. GC: Charles Ruggles (Lowell Redlings Farquhar), Arthur Gould Porter (Ravenswood).

119. Mr. Farquhar Stays On

When Mr. Farquhar asks Granny to go to Las Vegas, she thinks he wants to elope, but what he really wants is to go on a gambling spree with her money. GC: Charles Ruggles (Farquhar).

120. Military School

The Clampett estate becomes a battlefield when Jethro enrolls in The Havenhurst Military Academy in Beverly Hills. GC: John Hoyt (Colonel Hollis), Craig Hundley (Cadet), John Reilly (Captain Hogan).

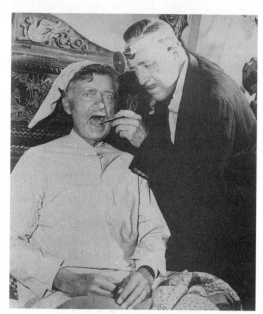

Dr. Roy Clyburn (Fred Clark) challenges Granny's
mountain medicine. *Viacom*

121. The Common Cold

Granny opens her own doctor's office when an M.D. refuses to believe
she has a cure for the common cold. GC: Fred Clark (Dr. Clyburn), Olan
Soule (Salesman), Tom Browne Henry (Parker), Lenore Kingston
(Receptionist).

122. The Richest Woman

The richest woman in the world meets some stiff opposition from Jed
when she insists on buying the Clampett mansion. GC: Martha Hyer
(Tracy Richards), Douglas Dumbrille (Doug).

123. The Trotting Horse

The Hillbillies are unimpressed with the champion harness-racing horse
Drysdale buys for them as an investment. GC: Norman Leavitt (Driver),
Herb Vigran (Handler).

124. The Buggy

Drysdale persuades his wife to accept Granny's challenge to a horse-and-
buggy race.

125. The Cat Burglar

A burglar on the loose in Beverly Hills tries to deceive the Clampetts before robbing their mansion. GC: John Ashley (Mike Wilcox), Norman Grabowski (Bernie).

126. The Big Chicken

Granny discovers an ostrich gulping tomatoes in her backyard and thinks it's a monstrous chicken. GC: John Baer (Nelson), Arthur Gould Porter (Ravenswood).

127. Sonny Drysdale Returns

Sonny Drysdale pays a return visit to Beverly Hills, rekindling the Clampetts' hope of a romance with Elly May. GC: Louis Nye (Sonny).

128. Brewster's Baby

Granny announces she is going back home on doctor business to "fetch" a baby into the world. GC: Lisa Seagram (Mrs. Brewster), Joyce Nizzari (Kitty Kat), Christine Williams (Girl), Frank Wilcox (Brewster).

129. The Great Jethro

A starving but flamboyant vaudeville magician meets Jethro and sees a chance to unload his old magic paraphernalia. GC: John Carradine (Marvo the Magnificent), Lennie Bremen (Truck driver), Britt Nilsson (1st Girl), Carolyn Williams (2nd Girl), Al Eben (Truck driver).

130. The Old Folks Home

Granny fears that the family is plotting to send her to an old folks' home when they suggest she'd be happier in a country cottage. GC: Edith Leslie (Mrs. Mack), Barney Elmore (Perkins).

131. Flatt and Scruggs Return

Country music stars Lester Flatt and Earl Scruggs return, and Jane becomes a folk singer. GC: Lester Flatt (Himself), Gladys Flatt (Joi Lansing), Earl Scruggs (Himself), Barney Elmore (Chauffeur).

132. The Folk Singers

Jethro abandons his career as an astronaut for the more precarious job of folksinger. GC: Tom D'Andrea (Kingsley), Venita Wolf (Miss Murray).

133. The Beautiful Maid
A glamorous Swedish actress who yearns to play a hillbilly moves in with the Clampetts to study backwoods dialect. GC: Julie Newmar (Ulla Bergstrom), Milton Frome (Chapman).

134. Jethro's Pad
Jethro concludes that he must have a cool bachelor pad in order to make a hit with women. GC: Bettina Brenna (Edy), Christine Williams (1st Kitty Kat), Phyllis Davis (2nd Kitty Kat).

135. The Bird-Watchers
The bird-watching Professor P. Caspar Biddle jeopardizes Elly May's romance with film star Dash Riprock. GC: Wally Cox (Professor Biddle), Venita Wolf (Miss Murray), Larry Pennell (Dash Riprock).

136. Jethro Gets Engaged
Jethro is sure he's going to be twice as big a movie star as Dash Riprock when he lands a job as Dash's double. GC: Joan Huntington (Debbie Haber), Pat Harrington (Phil Gordon), Dick Winslow (Man), Larry Pennell (Dash Riprock), Ray Kellogg (Guard).

137. Granny Tonics a Bird-Watcher
Professor P. Caspar Biddle, the meek little leader of Biddle's Bird-Watchers, guzzles Granny's annual spring tonic and turns into a tiger. GC: Wally Cox (Professor Biddle), Venita Wolf (Miss Murray).

138. Jethro Goes to College
Jethro decides he's ready for college and enrolls in the only one that will accept him—a run-down secretarial school. GC: Louise Lorimer (Dean Frisby), Gloria Neil (Miss Plumpett), Hope Summers (Miss Pringle), Shuji J. Nozawa (Hoshu Fujiyama).

139. The Party Line
Granny demands a party-line phone in Beverly Hills, so she can listen in. GC: Vinton Hayworth (Cramer).

140. The Soup Contest
Granny hopes to win Elly May a husband by entering an old hillbilly recipe in a contest and signing Elly May's name to it. GC: Gavin Gordon

Granny brings a tellee-phone from back home and demands a party line be installed just for her nosy pleasure. *Courtesy of Personality Photos, Inc.*

(Stafford Clark), Steve Dunne (Roger Dickerback), Steve Pendleton (Director).

141. Jethro Takes Love Lessons

Jethro falls for a waitress who gives him the brush-off until she learns he's a friend of handsome movie idol Dash Riprock. GC: Larry Pennell (Dash Riprock), Carol Booth (Susie).

142. The Badger Game

Blackmailers use hidden photographic and recording devices to trap unsuspecting Jed Clampett. GC: Leon Ames (Colonel Foxhall), Gayle Hunnicutt (Emaline Fetty).

143. The Badgers Return

Having failed in their attempt to fleece Jed Clampett, a pair of blackmailers turn their attention to Drysdale. GC: Leon Ames (Foxhall), David Frankham (Lieutenant Richards), Gayle Hunnicutt (Emaline).

144. The Gorilla

Jethro and Elly May want a gorilla, so Jed decides to order one up from Mr. Drysdale. Trying to discourage them, Drysdale has a friend dress in a gorilla costume to intimidate and frighten the Clampetts. GC: George Barrows (Gorilla).

Granny tries to domesticate a "go-rilla" with a sweat and a switch.

Courtesy of Personality Photos, Inc.

145. Come Back, Little Herby
The Clampetts beg Drysdale to get Herby, their domesticated gorilla, back. GC: George Barrows (Gorilla).

146. Jed in Politics
Jed runs for Beverly Hills Smog Commissioner when the incumbent stops Granny from cooking up her smog-producing homemade lye soap. GC: Paul Reed (Russell Tinsley).

147. Clampett Cha Cha Cha
Marvin and Marita introduce the Clampetts to the art of terpsichore and try to run a fake dance school out of the Clampetts' mansion. GC: Frank Faylen (Marvin), Iris Adrian (Marita).

148. Jed Joins the Board
Millionaire Jed Clampett finds a job as a garbage collector because he's weary of being useless. Drysdale persuades him to take a seat on the board of directors of the O.K. Oil Company. GC: Frank Wilcox (Brewster), Owen Cunningham (Director), Jack Grinnage (Copilot), Jan

Arvan (Forbes), Barry Kelly (Brachner), Tommy Farrell (Pilot), Lindsay Workman (Peterson).

149. Granny Lives It Up
Granny is pursued simultaneously by two elderly men—both after her money. GC: Diane Farrell (Page girl), Jo Ann Pflug (1st Girl), Anne Newman (2nd Girl), Roy Roberts (Cushing), Charles Ruggles (Farquhar).

150. The Gloria Swanson Story
The Clampetts arrange a career comeback for an idol of the silent screen who they think is destitute. GC: Gloria Swanson (Herself), George Neise (Auctioneer), Lennie Bremen (1st Mover), Frank Sully (2nd Mover), Milton Frome (Chapman), Ray Kellogg (Guard).

151. The Woodchucks
Jethro tries to join Biddle's Bird-Watchers after he spots a beauty in the ranks of the for-women-only club. GC: Nancy Dow (Athena), Sandy Berke (Lolita), Jerry Rannow (Stanley), Twila Anderson, Holly Matthews, Giovanna Coppola, Penny Antine, Lavina Dawson, and Lynn Ketchum (Birdwatchers).

152. Foggy Mountain Soap
Flatt and Scruggs make their fifth annual appearance. Recognizing the homespun sincerity of Jed and Granny, an advertising man persuades Flatt, Scruggs, Granny, and Jed to appear in a television soap commercial. GC: Lester Flatt and Earl Scruggs (Themselves), Bob Watson (Harry Hogan), Tom Curtis (Makeup man), Edward Andrews (Stewart), Terry Phillips (Sound man).

153. The Christmas Present
The Clampetts work as temporary Christmas help in a department store. GC: James Millhollin (Manager), Bruce Hyde (Floorwalker), Dee Carroll (Woman).

154. The Flying Saucer
Drysdale hires three Italian midgets—the Montenaro brothers—to dress as men from outer space in a scheme to get publicity for his bank. The Clampetts think Martians have invaded. GC: Frank Delfino (1st Mon-

Midget Billy Curtis plays a little actor in a Martian costume whom Drysdale has hired for a promotion. Granny is convinced he's one of them "little green goomers from Mars." *Author's collection*

tenaro), Jerry Maren (2nd Montenaro), Billy Curtis (3rd Montenaro), John Alvin (Photograher). The Montenaro characters were named after the show's property man, Joe Montenaro.

155. The Mayor of Bug Tussle

The Clampetts are honored by a distinguished visitor from home—the mayor of Bug Tussle. GC: James Westerfield (Mayor Amos Wentworth Hogg).

156. Granny Retires

Drysdale panics when Granny says that she's going to withdraw her $15 million from his bank and go back to the hills. GC: Fred Clark (Dr. Clyburn).

157. The Clampett Curse

Granny convinces Jed that money is a curse, so Jed gives away his entire fortune to three struggling college girls. GC: Sheila James (Ginny Jennings), Bernadette Withers (Lucy), Toby Kaye (Fran), Russ Grieve (Ranger Warkle).

On the alert in "The Indians Are Coming." *CBS/Fox Video*

158. The Indians Are Coming
When some Indian landowners come to reconcile a boundary dispute with Jed, Granny thinks they are on the warpath and prepares for war. GC: John Wayne (Himself), John Considine (Little Fox), Stanley Waxman (Chief Running Wolf), Milton Frome (Chapman), Vince St. Cyr (Indian).

159. The Marriage Machine
The Hillbillies attempt computer dating, but misunderstand the choices of the computer matchmaker. Jed winds up with Jethro's girlfriend and vice-versa. GC: Warrene King (Linda Oliver), Richard Collier (Filbert), Larry Christman (Hugh), Lurene Tuttle (Gladys Peabody), John Ayres (Bert).

160. Elly Comes Out
Jed and Granny throw a "comin'-out" party for Elly May, and Mrs. Drysdale plots to make the affair a fiasco. GC: Jenifer Lea (Secretary), Robert Strauss (Society Sandy).

161. The Matador
After watching women surround El Magnifico, the world's greatest matador, jealous Jethro takes up bullfighting. GC: Milton Frome (Chapman), Kay St. Germain (Secretary), Miguel Landa (El Magnifico).

162. The Gypsy's Warning

Mrs. Drysdale hires a pair of fortune-tellers to frighten the Clampetts out of Beverly Hills with dire prophecies. GC: Leon Belasco (Yerko), Bella Bruck (Narda).

163. His Royal Highness

Ex-King Alexander of Sabalia tries to marry wealthy Elly May because he hasn't a nickel to his name. GC: Jacques Bergerac (King Alexander), Edward Ashley (Man on yacht), Victoria Carroll (Doreen).

164. Super Hawg

Granny stumbles upon a hippopotamus that Drysdale has acquired for an advertising scheme and thinks it's a giant hog. Granny wants to butcher it for ham.

165. The Doctors

It's spring again and Granny tries to dispense her free tonic at the bank, resulting in another run-in with Dr. Clyburn and another TV commercial. GC: Barbara Morrison (Mrs. De Longpre), Fred Clark (Dr. Clyburn), Lorraine Bendix (Miss Lovely).

166. Delovely and Scruggs

Lester Flatt and Earl Scruggs revisit the Clampetts and Mrs. Flatt wants to get into acting, so Jethro directs her in a screen test. GC: Lester Flatt and Earl Scruggs (Themselves), Joi Lansing (Gladys Flatt), Bobs Watson (Harry Hogan), John Alvin (Photographer).

167. The Little Monster

Drysdale's precocious eleven-year-old nephew swindles the Hillbillies out of all the valuable art objects in their mansion. GC: Ted Eccles (Milby Drysdale).

168. The Dahlia Feud

Mrs. Drysdale's attempt to grow prize-winning dahlias renews her feud with Granny. Granny thinks Mrs. Drysdale has hired a hit man. GC: Ted Cassidy (Mr. Ted, the gardener).

Granny is a royal "oaf" and Jed is the Earl of
Clampett. *Courtesy of Personality Photos, Inc.*

169. Jed Inherits a Castle

The Clampetts learn that they have inherited a castle and The Earl of
Clampett and his kin prepare for a journey to Britain. GC: Paul Lynde
(Passport clerk).

170. The Clampetts in London

The Clampetts arrive in London, where Granny encounters difficulty
with both the customs inspector and an English pharmacist. GC: Shary
Marshall (Stewardess), Ernest Clarke (Giles-Evans), John Orchard (Customs inspector), Alan Napier (Chemist), Larry Blake (Cabdriver), Hugh
Dempster (Cholmondeley), John Baron (Chauffeur).

171. Clampett Castle

The Clampetts arrive at their inherited English castle, confusion reigns,
and Jethro insists on acting like a medieval knight in search of a dragon.
GC: John Baron (Chauffeur), Norman Claridge (Jenkins), Elaine
Stevens (Maid), Richard Caldicot (John Faversham), Ernest Clarke
(Giles-Evans), Sheila Fearn (Young lady).

172. Robin Hood of Griffith Park

The Clampetts pay the $10 million tax on their castle in England, turn the place over to the staff, and leave for home. Jethro feels jilted, goes berserk, and wants to play Robin Hood in nearby Griffith Park. GC: Laurel Goodwin (Stella), Richard Caldicot (Faversham), John Baron (Chauffeur), Alan Reed, Jr. (Buddy), Norman Claridge (Jenkins).

173. Robin Hood and the Sheriff

Jethro continues to masquerade as the Robin Hood of Griffith Park and becomes a charismatic leader of a hippy cult. GC: Laurel Goodwin (Stella), Christian Anderson (Harold), Paul De Rolf (Paul), Pat McCaffrie (Fred), Alan Reed, Jr. (Buddy), Carolyn Williamson (Ruthie), Victor French (Tony), The Peppermint Trolley Company (the Singers). *Note:* The Peppermint Trolley Company was an upbeat bubblegum pop chorus that sang the original "Brady Bunch" theme song in the show's first season. (They were later replaced by the Brady kids from the show.)

174. Greetings from the President

When Jethro gets his draft notice, he buys himself a surplus army tank and a general's uniform and begins his own training. GC: Bea Benaderet (Cousin Pearl), Pat McCaffrie (Fred), Henry Corden (Charley).

175. The Army Game

Draftee Jethro's military career comes to a halt when army psychiatrists refuse to believe his family is for real. GC: Paul Reed (Colonel Stark), Joe Conley (Sergeant), King Donovan (Psychiatrist).

176. Mr. Universe Muscles In

A rival banker arranges a date for Elly May with a handsome model, so Drysdale counters by furnishing "Mr. Universe" (Dave Draper) as an escort. GC: Dave Draper (Himself), Roy Roberts (John Cushing), John Ashley (Troy Apollo).

177. A Plot for Granny

Two confused salesmen attempt to sell Jed a cemetery plot for Granny, but Jed thinks he's buying her a piece of land to farm. GC: Richard Deacon (Brubaker), Jesse White (Mortimer).

178. The Social Climbers

The Clampetts entertain a lady blacksmith from back home who was the social queen of the hills. GC: Mary Wickes (Adaline Ashley), Gail Bonney (Mrs. Robinson).

179. Jethro's Military Career

Bent on a military career, Jethro experiments with underwater demolition while practicing to be a navy frogman in the swimming pool. Granny thinks there is a "creature" in the cee-ment pond.

180. The Reserve Program

When Granny spies a group of movie actors dressed as Union soldiers from the Civil War, she prepares to go to war with them. GC: Lyle Talbot (Colonel Blake), Bob Pickett (Lieutenant), Harry Fleer (Colonel), Ron Stokes (Sergeant O'Hara), William Mims (General Grant), Steve Thomas (Major).

181. The South Rises Again

Granny recruits her own commandos against the Union when she thinks battle scenes for a Civil War movie are the real thing. GC: Lyle Talbot

Granny insists that Jefferson Davis was the greatest president who ever lived.
Courtesy of Personality Photos, Inc.

"*I do* declare!" Granny models her Southern best.

Courtesy of Kingsley Colton

(Colonel Blake), Harry Fleer (Colonel), Richard O'Shea (Sergeant), Harry Lauter (Captain), William Mims (General Grant), Terry Phillips (Foster Phinney). *Note:* The real Foster Phinney was the show's assistant director.

182. Jethro in the Reserves
Granny thinks she has captured aged General Ulysses S. Grant and sets out to woo him by donning a bathing suit. GC: Lyle Talbot (Colonel Blake), William Mims (General Grant).

183. Cimarron Drip
Jethro can't get himself a part in a television series, but Bessie, Elly May's pet chimp, wins the starring role. GC: Larry Pennell (Dash Riprock), Theodore Marcuse (Von Schlepper), Milton Frome (Larry Chapman), Jim Hayward (Maintenance man).

184. Corn Pone Picassos

Granny paints a picture to help Mrs. Drysdale win the Beverly Hill Culture Committee Award. GC: David Bond (Judge Curtis), Chet Stratton (A. Allen Allen), Frank Richards (Truck driver).

185. The Clampetts Play Cupid

Granny quits trying to persuade Elly May to marry movie star Dash Riprock and decides to help Jane Hathaway nab him. GC: Larry Pennell (Dash Riprock), Valerie Hawkins (Camille).

186. The Housekeeper

Despite Granny's protests, Jed and Mr. Drysdale hire a housekeeper who quickly gets on Granny's nerves. GC: Fran Ryan (Miss Meek).

187. The Diner

When Jed Clampett decides to set his nephew up in the restaurant business, Jethro becomes the operator of a dilapidated diner (The Happy Gizzard). GC: Joan Huntington (Lois).

188. Topless Anyone?

Jethro thinks a "topless" policy for the diner might bring in customers. He assumes "topless" means without a hat. GC: Ysabel MacCloskey (Mrs. Vanderpont), James F. Stone (Mr. Vanderpont), Robert Foulk (Truck driver), Venita Wolf (Suzy).

189. The Great Snow

Granny gets homesick for a good snowstorm and Mr. Drysdale arranges for a blizzard to hit Beverly Hills. GC: Bill Baldwin (Announcer's voice).

190. The Rass'lin Clampetts

Granny's inflamed by a woman's wrestling match on television and she joins the tag-team match. GC: Jerry Randall (in drag as the Boston Strong Girl), Gene LeBell (Referee), Bill Baldwin (Announcer), Gayle Caldwell (Rebecca).

191. The Great Tag-Team Match

The Hillbillies gird for a tag-team wrestling match after Granny defeats the Boston Strong Girl. GC: Alan Reed (Gene Booth), Jerry Randall (in drag as the Boston Strong Girl), Kay St. Germain (Secretary), Mike

Granny gets a stronghold on her opponent (Mike
Mazurki) in a tag-team match. *CBS/Fox Video*

Mazurki (Wrestler), Gayle Caldwell (Rebecca), Bill Baldwin
(Announcer), Gene LeBell (Referee), Merie Earle (Rebecca's mother),
Margo Epper (Boston Strong Girl's mother). *Note:* Jerry Brutsche, Irene
Ryan's longtime stunt double, played Granny *and* Rebecca's father.

192. Jethro Proposes

Granny feels sorry about the lack of romance in Jane Hathaway's life, so
she forces Jethro to propose, expecting Jane to refuse. GC: Lisa Todd
(Ilse), Fritz Feld (Waiter).

Granny disguises herself to eavesdrop during Jethro and Miss Jane's romantic dinner
in the episode "Jethro Proposes." *Courtesy of Personality Photos, Inc.*

The Beverly Hillbillies

193. The Clampetts Fiddle Around
Drysdale hires Sebastian Stromboli, the world's greatest violin virtuoso, to teach Jethro to play the fiddle. GC: Hans Conried (Stromboli), Foster Brooks ("Fiddlin' Sam").

194. The Soap Opera
Granny thinks a television soap opera is real and sets out to rescue a patient who is about to undergo a serious operation. GC: Grandon Rhodes (Doctor), Beecey Carlson (Maggie), John Dehner (Rex Goodbody).

195. Dog Days
Granny becomes enraged when Elly May's herd of animals tramples her every time she calls dinner. GC: Lisa Todd (Ilse), Terry Phillips (Wolf), Paul DeRolf (Wolf).

196. The Crystal Gazers
Granny convinces herself that she has the gift of prophecy and starts making doubtful predictions for her family and friends. GC: Connie Sawyer (Elverna Bradshaw). *Note:* For just this episode, another actress replaced Elvia Allman in the role of Elverna Bradshaw.

197. From Rags to Riches
Granny prepares to perform history's first surgical head transplant when Drysdale is hurt in a fracas with his wife. GC: Carolyn Nelson (Secretary).

Drysdale films a commercial casting Elly May and Granny as its stars in the episode "From Rags to Riches." *Courtesy of Personality Photos, Inc.*

198. Cousin Roy

Cousin Roy Halsey arrives from the hills as advance man for Granny's hated rival, Myrtle Halsey, noted distiller of "medicine." GC: Roy Clark (Roy Halsey/Mother Myrtle), Phil Arnold (Maintenance man), Peter Leeds (Policeman). Note: Halsey is actually the last name of Roy Clark's manager.

199. A Bundle for Britain

Jed decides to withdraw his $80 million from Drysdale's bank and give it to "poverty-stricken" England. GC: Richard Caldicot (Faversham), Ben Wrigley (Footman), Alan Mowbray (Montrose).

200. Something for the Queen

The Clampetts invade England again to return Canada (which they have purchased) to the Queen. GC: Richard Caldicot (Faversham), Warrene Ott (Stewardess), Dick Wesson (Man on plane), Mark Harris (Customs inspector), Jack Bannon (Customs assistant), Brian Peck (Chauffeur), Alistair Williamson (Doorman), Donald Bisset (Tetley).

201. War of the Roses

Drysdale orders Jane Hathaway to pose as Queen Elizabeth I, who the Hillbillies think still rules England. GC: Richard Caldicot (Faversham), Sydney Arnold (Retainer), Rosalind Knight (Vanessa), William Kendall (Colonel Dumbarton), Donald Bisset (Tetley), Peter Myers (Osgood).

202. Coming Through the Rye

Jethro falls for a beautiful Scot, but his Hillbilly kin confuse her with her hulking brother in a kilt. GC: Richard Caldicot (Faversham), Ilona Rodgers (Sandy), William Kendall (Colonel Dumbarton), Dave Prowse (Emlyn), Brian Peck (Chauffeur).

203. Ghost of Clampett Castle

Drysdale arranges for a "ghost" to scare the Clampetts out of their English castle so they'll return to Beverly Hills. GC: Richard Caldicot (Faversham).

204. Granny Goes to Hooterville

Granny plans a trip to Hooterville but gets sidetracked when she thinks that Jed is planning to marry Jane Hathaway. GC: Edgar Buchanan (Joe Carson), Aron Kincaid (Cliff), Frank Cady (Sam Drucker).

205. The Italian Cook

Jethro hires a chef, a gorgeous Italian girl who cooks masterfully but doesn't speak a word of English. GC: Maria Mirka (Maria), Mike Minor (Steve Elliott), Linda Kaye Henning (Betty Jo), Frank Cady (Sam Drucker), Dick O'Shea (Pilot).

206. The Great Cook-Off

Jethro begins dressing and acting like the noblest Roman of them all to win the hand of Maria, the beautiful Italian cook. GC: Maria Mirka (Maria).

207. Bonnie, Flatt, and Scruggs

The Hillbillies get to play the part of gangsters when Mr. Drysdale makes a commercial film for his bank. GC: Lester Flatt and Earl Scruggs (Themselves), Joi Lansing (Gladys Flatt), Percy Helton (Homer Cratchit).

208. The Thanksgiving Spirit

The Hillbillies travel to Hooterville to spend the holiday with their friends from "Petticoat Junction" and "Green Acres." GC: Lori Saunders (Bobbie Jo), Linda Kaye Henning (Betty Jo), Frank Cady (Sam Drucker), Eddie Albert (Oliver Douglas), Eva Gabor (Lisa Douglas), Tom Lester (Eb),

Henning Hall of Fame: This rare portrait captures the casts of "The Beverly Hillbillies," "Petticoat Junction," and "Green Acres" for a Thanksgiving episode. Left to right: Max Baer, Meredith MacRae, Eddie Albert, Lori Saunders, Irene Ryan, Frank Cady, Nancy Kulp, Linda Kaye Henning, Buddy Ebsen, Donna Douglas, Mike Minor, Eva Gabor, June Lockhart, Tom Lester, Edgar Buchanan, and Raymond Bailey. *Photograph by Gabi Rona*

Edgar Buchanan (Uncle Joe), Meredith MacRae (Billie Jo), Mike Minor (Steve), June Lockhart (Dr. Janet Craig).

209. The Courtship of Homer Noodleman
Drysdale has Dash Riprock pose as farmboy Homer Noodleman to try to win Elly May. GC: Frank Cady (Sam Drucker), Larry Pennell (Dash Riprock), Tom Lester (Eb), Georgene Barnes (Jeanie), Donna Jean Young (Girl).

210. The Hot Rod Truck
Jethro tells Jed and Granny they're no longer "with it" and trades the old family jalopy for a new and powerful hot rod. GC: Georgene Barnes (Jeanie), Lonnie Burr (Medicine man).

211. The Week Before Christmas
The Hillbillies head back to Hooterville for Christmas—and a possible wedding for Granny and Sam Drucker. GC: Lori Saunders (Bobbie Jo), Frank Cady (Sam Drucker), Meredith MacRae (Billie Jo).

Jethro soups up the old truck for somethin' more akin to his "sophisticated Hollywood playboy" image.

Viacom

212. Christmas in Hooterville

The Hillbillies spend the Christmas holiday in Hooterville, where Eb courts Elly May and Granny pursues Sam Drucker. GC: Edgar Buchanan (Uncle Joe), Mike Minor (Steve), Meredith MacRae (Billie Jo), Tom Lester (Eb), Linda Kaye Henning (Betty Jo), Lori Saunders (Bobbie Jo), Frank Cady (Sam Drucker), Percy Helton (Homer Cratchit).

213. Drysdale and Friend

Drysdale is jailed for transporting Granny's white lightnin' and Elly May's drunken grizzly bear in Jethro's truck. GC: Percy Helton (Homer Cratchit), Stacy King (Kathy), Frank Cady (Sam Drucker), Mike Ross (Sheriff), J. Pat O'Malley (Judge), Hank Patterson (Fred Ziffel), George Dunn (Bailiff), Hank Worden (Harry).

214. Problem Bear

Drysdale comes down with the flu, and "Doctor" Granny tries to treat him with her moonshine. GC: Norma Varden (Mrs. Van Ransonhoff).

215. Jethro the Flesh Peddler

Jethro sets himself up in an office in the fifth floor of Drysdale's bank building as a Hollywood talent agent. GC: Pamela Rodgers (Bunny), Roy Clark (Cousin Roy), Judy Jordan (Chauffeur).

216. Cousin Roy in Movieland

Jethro rejects Cousin Roy as a client for his new Hollywood talent agency. GC: Pamela Rodgers (Bunny), Roy Clark (Cousin Roy), Judy Jordan (Chauffeur).

217. Jed Clampett Enterprises

Drysdale finally gets a paying tenant for the fifth floor of his bank building—by evicting Jethro and renting it to Jed. GC: Venita Wolf (Suzy), Jeannette O'Connor (Lee), Percy Helton (Homer Cratchit), Judy Jordan (Chauffeur), Seamon Glass (Julie).

218. The Phantom Fifth Floor

A building inspector probes the strange and assorted Jed Clampett enterprises on the fifth floor of Drysdale's bank building. GC: Herb Vigran (Armstrong), Seamon Glass (Julie).

219. The Hired Gun

Drysdale hires troubleshooter Homer Bedloe to evict the Clampetts from the Commerce Bank building's fifth floor. GC: Charles Lane (Homer Bedloe), Percy Helton (Homer Cratchit).

220. The Happy Bank

A beautiful secretary at Drysdale's bank purposely breaks the heel of her shoe and hobbles to "cobbler" Jed Clampett for a lift. GC: Percy Helton (Homer Cratchit), Judy Jordan (Babs), Ingeborg Kjeldsen (Carol), Georgene Barnes (Jeanie), Jeannette O'Connor (Linda), Dee Carroll (Pregnant woman).

221. Sam Drucker's Visit

Sam Drucker from Hooterville wins a trip to Hollywood, and Granny assumes that he's come to propose to her. GC: Larry Pennell (Dash Riprock), Lori Saunders (Bobbie Jo), Frank Cady (Sam Drucker), Allison McKay (Telegraph girl).

222. The Guru

Jethro reads a book about yoga and decides to become a guru, much to Granny's disgust. GC: Ray Kellogg (Policeman), William Mims (Guru).

223. The Jogging Clampetts

When the Clampetts take up jogging as a hobby, Mr. Drysdale puts on a jogging suit to trot along and seek new business for his bank. GC: Paul Newlan (Jason Detweiler).

224. Collard Greens an' Fatback

The Drysdales sell their mansion to singer Pat Boone, who is intrigued by Granny's steaming backyard kettle of hillbilly stew. GC: Pat Boone (Himself), Tris Coffin (Mr. Tucker), Jack Bannon (Policeman). *Note:* Pat Boone sings "Never Goin' Back to Nashville."

225. Back to the Hills

The Hillbillies move back to the hills to find Elly May a husband, but Jethro stays in Beverly Hills. GC: Rob Reiner (Mitch), B. Robert Corff (1st Student), Bonnie Boland (2nd Student).

Elverna Bradshaw (Elvia Allman) is infuriated by the
caricature rendered by her archrival, Granny.

Courtesy of Personality Photos, Inc.

226. The Hills of Home

The Clampetts arrive in the mountain town of Silver Dollar City,
where Granny starts a feud with an old rival, Elverna Bradshaw. GC:
Walter Woolf King (Parnell), Elvia Allman (Elverna Bradshaw), Lloyd
Heller (Shad), George "Shug" Fisher (Shorty), Rob Reiner (Mitch), B.
Robert Corff (Hippie), Bonnie Boland (Hippie), Wini Wesson (Miss
Walsh).

227. Silver Dollar City Fair

Granny continues her efforts to get Elly May married, extolling the
young girl's virtues to every bachelor she meets. GC: Elvia Allman
(Elverna), Lloyd Heller (Shad), Shug Fisher (Shorty), Chick Allen
(Himself), Slim Wilson (Man), Delores Stroud (Woman), Jerry Brutsche
(Telegraph man), Paul de Rolf (Man), Hope Wainwright (Stewardess).

228. Jane Finds Elly a Man
Bird-watcher Jane Hathaway hikes into the woods and finds a 6'6" man for Elly May. GC: Shug Fisher (Shorty), Elvia Allman (Elverna), Roger Torrey (Matthew Templeton), Eck Boseman (Himself), Jerry Brutsche (Holloway).

229. Wedding Plans
The Clampetts rehearse for Elly May's wedding to backwoodsman Matthew Templeton, unaware that he is already married. GC: Shug Fisher (Shorty), Elvia Allman (Elverna), Roger Torrey (Matthew), Jerry Brutsche (Holloway).

230. Jed Buys Central Park
Elly May's wedding is called off, so Jed plans to buy Central Park and move the family to New York to find her a man there. GC: Phil Silvers (Shifty Shafer, aka "Honest John"), Elvia Allman (Elverna), Jerry Brutsche (Holloway), Shug Fisher (Shorty), Roger Torrey (Matthew), Pat Winters (Stewardess). *Note:* Shug Fisher also plays the scraggly farmer.

231. The Clampetts in New York
Con man Shifty Shafer sells Central Park to the Clampetts and then unloads three other New York landmarks on them. GC: Phil Silvers (Shifty), John Cliff (Policeman), Norman Grabowski (1st Mugger), Bucklind Berry (2nd Mugger), Dick Wesson (Cabbie), Peggy Russell (Old woman).

232. Manhattan Hillbillies
Drysdale and Jane arrive in New York in an attempt to locate and persuade the Hillbillies to abandon their half-built cabin in Central Park and return home. GC: Sammy Davis, Jr. (Sergeant Patrick Muldoon), Norman Grabowski (1st Mugger), Bucklind Berry (2nd Mugger), Lennie Bremen (Cabbie), Sean McClory (Policeman).

233. Home Again
Granny insists she doesn't need glasses, although she carries on a conversation with a pet seal, thinking it's Elly's new boyfriend. GC: Brian West (Dr. Bob Graham), John Scott Lindsey (Jimmy), Judy McConnell (Secretary).

234. Shorty Kellems Moves West
Shorty Kellems, proprietor of the hotel in Silver Dollar City, sells out and leaves the hills to join the Clampetts in California. GC: Judy Jordan (Miss Switzer), Shug Fisher (Shorty), Judy McConnell (Miss Leeds), Gloria Hill (Tall woman), Lisa Britton and Ruth Ko (Belly dancers).

235. Midnight Shorty
Drysdale, trying to get Shorty to deposit money in his bank, taunts the visiting mountaineer with girls and games. GC: Shug Fisher (Shorty), Danielle Mardi (Miss Thompson), Judy Jordan (Miss Switzer), Bettina Brenna (Miss Buckles), Judy McConnell (Miss Leeds), Ruth Ko (Dealer).

236. Shorty Go Home
Granny uses her shotgun as she punishes Jethro for leading too wild a Hollywood life with Shorty Kellems. GC: Shug Fisher (Shorty), Danielle Mardi (Miss Thompson), Judy Jordan (Miss Switzer), Bettina Brenna (Miss Buckles), Judy McConnell (Miss Leeds).

237. The Hero
Mrs. Drysdale gives her nephew, who has just left the air force, a hero's welcome and a job as vice president at Commerce Bank. GC: Soupy Sales (Lance Bradford), Danielle Mardi (1st Girl), Ruth Ko (2nd Girl), Gloria Hill (3rd Girl), Carolyn Williamson (4th Girl).

238. Our Hero the Banker
Mrs. Drysdale's nephew, who possesses a wealth of confidence but no talent, takes over Drysdale's private office at the Commerce Bank. GC: Soupy Sales (Lance Bradford), Judy Jordan (Miss Switzer), Danielle Mardi (Miss Thompson), Devon Blaine (Miss Butterfield), Mady Maguire (Miss Graham).

239. Buzz Bodine, Boy General
The Clampetts visit Hooterville and Jed arranges to go into the airline business with pilot Steve Elliott. GC: Mike Minor (Steve Elliot), Linda Kaye Henning (Betty Jo Elliott), Frank Cady (Sam Drucker), Guy Raymond (Howard Hewes).

240. The Clampett-Hewes Empire

Drysdale eagerly prepares to set up the deal for a new airline formed by Jed and farmer Howard Hewes, mistaking Hewes for famous industrial billionaire Howard Hughes in a phone conversation with Jed. GC: Guy Raymond (Howard Hewes), Winifred Coffin (Mrs. Hewes), Linda Kaye Henning (Betty Jo), Mike Minor (Steve Elliott), Frank Cady (Sam Drucker), Judy Jordan, Mady Maguire, and Danielle Mardi (Secretaries).

241. What Happened to Shorty?

Jed Clampett and Silver Dollar City's Shad Heller conspire to line up Shorty Kellems as a husband for the strong-minded widow Elverna Bradshaw. GC: Shug Fisher (Shorty), Shad Heller (Shad), Elvia Allman (Elverna), Bettina Brenna (Gloria Buckles).

242. Marry Me Shorty

The Hillbillies again conspire to get Shorty married to Elverna. This time, Drysdale converts his bank office into an Arabian harem chamber for a wild bachelor's party. GC: Shug Fisher (Shorty), Shad Heller (Shad), Elvia Allman (Elverna), Bettina Brenna (Gloria Buckles), Danielle Mardi (Helen), Ruth Ko (Exotic dancer), Susan Harris (Harem girl), Jean Bell, Diana Bartlett, and Devon Blaine (Slavegirls).

243. Shorty Spits the Hook

Elusive Shorty Kellems gets off the marital hook by convincing Elverna that he's a maniacal gambler. GC: Shug Fisher (Shorty), Shad Heller (Shad), Elvia Allman (Elverna), Cookie Gilchrist (Cookie), Earl Faison (Earl), Diana Bartlett, Devon Blaine, and Jean Bell (Slavegirls/Secretaries). *Note:* Two ex-pro football players, Cookie Gilchrist and Earl Faison, play the brothers of one of the secretaries in this episode.

244. Three-Day Reprieve

Jed and Shad Heller discover it's a full-time job keeping Shorty corralled until his marriage to the indomitable Elverna. GC: Shug Fisher (Shorty), Shad Heller (Shad), Elvia Allman (Elverna), Jean Bell (Sugar), Johnny Williams (Guard), Mary Akins (Faith), Vikki Bandlow (Grace), Elena Luck (Joy).

245. The Wedding
Shorty Kellems again short-circuits Elverna's wedding plans, this time by marrying Mr. Drysdale's prettiest secretary. GC: Shug Fisher (Shorty), Elvia Allman (Elverna), Bettina Brenna (Gloria), Vincent Perry (Judge Marshall), Kim Brewer (Hope).

246. Annul That Marriage
The Clampetts set up a miniature farm so Shorty's bride, Gloria, can sample farm life, and soon the exhausted girl is delighted to find out she's not really married. GC: Shug Fisher (Shorty), Elvia Allman (Elverna), Bettina Brenna (Gloria).

247. Hotel for Women
The Hillbillies leave Shorty Kellems temporarily in charge of the Clampett mansion, and he turns it into a hotel for single secretaries. GC: Shug Fisher (Shorty), Bettina Brenna (Gloria), Jean Bell (Jean), Danielle Mardi, Devon Blaine, Ruth Ko, and Sheila Leighton (Secretaries).

248. Simon Legree Drysdale
The Clampett mansion is set up as a hotel for women, and Drysdale decides to extort a few dollars from his secretary guests. GC: Jean Bell (Jean), Danielle Mardi (Helen Thompson), Diana Bartlette (Joy Devine), Cookie Gilchrest (Cookie), Earl Faison (Earl), Barney Elmore (Chauffeur).

249. Honest John Returns
The Hillbillies again meet "Honest John," the con man who had sold them half of Manhattan and then mysteriously returned their money. GC: Phil Silvers (Honest John/Shifty), Kathleen Freeman (Flo).

250. Honesty is The Best Policy
Jed prepares to underwrite Honest John's scheme to drill a channel in the mountains to draw off Los Angeles's smog. GC: Phil Silvers (Honest John/Shifty), Kathleen Freeman (Flo), Dave Willock (Fred Hutchins).

251. The Pollution Solution
The Hillbillies plan to go to Washington to give the President their $95 million fortune to help fight air pollution. GC: Rich Little (Himself), Bill Beckett (Milkman).

252. The Clampetts in Washington

The Clampetts arrive in Washington, D.C., to sightsee and to give the President $95 million to help in the fight against smog. GC: Phil Silvers (Shifty Shafer), Keith Rogers (Stewardess), Richard Erdman (Guard), Kathleen Freeman (Flo Shafer), Al Lanti (Cabdriver).

253. Jed Buys the Capitol

Shifty Shafer sells Jed the Capitol building, the Pentagon, the Lincoln Memorial, the zoo, and various other choice pieces of Washington real estate. GC: Phil Silvers (Shifty), Kathleen Freeman (Flo), Cliff Norton (Waiter).

254. Mark Templeton Arrives

Romance enters Elly May's life when navy lieutenant Mark Templeton (twin brother of Matthew Templeton, the Ozark preacher) arrives at the Clampett mansion to pay a visit. GC: Roger Torrey (Mark Templeton), Sherry Miles (Darlene Mattingly).

255. Don't Marry a Frogman

Granny is convinced that Elly May's navy frogman boyfriend is actually a half-human amphibian. GC: Roger Torrey (Mark Templeton).

256. Doctor, Cure My Frog

Granny consults a psychiatrist to give "a city doctor" a chance to keep frogman Mark Templeton from turning into a real frog. GC: Roger Torrey (Mark Templeton), Richard Deacon (Dr. Klingner).

257. Do You, Elly, Take This Frog?

Granny takes a sleeping potion and has a nightmare that Elly May marries a "giant frog." GC: Roger Torrey (Mark Templeton), Vincent Perry (Judge Marshall), Richard Deacon (Dr. Klingner).

258. The Frog Family

Granny battles to keep her family out of the swimming pool, convinced that if they get wet they'll turn into frogs. GC: Roger Torrey (Mark Templeton), Richard Deacon (Dr. Klingner).

259. Farm in the Ocean

Frogman Mark Templeton unsuccessfully tries to convince Granny that man's future lies on the ocean floor. GC: Roger Torrey (Mark Templeton), Richard Deacon (Dr. Klingner), Warrene Ott (Sharon Klingner).

260. Shorty to the Rescue

Granny sends back home to the hills for Shorty Kellems to help break up Elly May's romance with Mark Templeton. GC: Roger Torrey (Mark Templeton), Shug Fisher (Shorty).

261. Welcome to the Family

Granny thinks Shorty Kellems has turned into a seal because he ignored her warnings about swimming in the Clampett pool. GC: Roger Torrey (Mark Templeton), Lori Saunders (Betty Gordon), Shug Fisher (Shorty).

262. The Great Revelation

Granny is finally convinced that Elly May's boyfriend, Mark Templeton, is a human being—not half frog, as she suspected. GC: Roger Torrey (Mark Templeton), Danielle Mardi (Helen Thompson).

263. The Grunion Invasion

Jed, Granny, Elly May, and Jethro prepare to go to war with the unwanted grunions, which they think are hostile people from another country invading California. GC: Danielle Mardi (Helen Thompson), Jerry Brutsche (Surfer), Sue Bernard (Girl).

264. The Girls from Grun

The Hillbillies, encouraged by Drysdale, continue to guard the Malibu beach and repel the mythical grunion invaders. GC: Danielle Mardi (Helen Thompson), David Moses (Medic), Sue Bernard (Girl), Jane Axell (Secretary), Jerry Brutsche (Surfer).

265. The Grun Incident

Drysdale's rebellious bank secretaries organize to fight for better wages and working conditions. GC: Danielle Mardi (Helen Thompson), Jane Axell (Ulla), Foster Brooks (Man), Francisco Ortega (Guard), Momo Yashima (1st Girl), Roberta Carol (2nd Girl).

266. Women's Lib

Granny and Elly May join the Women's Liberation Movement and leave all household chores to Jed and Jethro; naturally, disaster results. GC: Danielle Mardi (Helen), Momo Yashima (Susie), Fuji (Banzai Sakito), Francisco Ortega (Guard).

267. The Teahouse of Jed Clampett

The Hillbilly womenfolk move in with Miss Jane, but Jed and Jethro replace them with a trio of Japanese beauties. GC: Charles Lane (Foster Phinney), Lori Saunders (Betty), Danielle Mardi (Helen), Fuji (Banzai Sakito), Momo Yashima, Sumi Haru, Kazuka Sakura, Miko Mayama (Japanese girls). *Note:* The character Foster Phinney was named after the show's assistant director, Foster Phinney.

268. The Palace of Clampett-San

Jed and Jethro enjoy an idyllic interval of living like Asian potentates, waited on hand and foot by three lovely Japanese women. GC: Charles Lane (Foster Phinney), Miko Mayama (Miko), Momo Yashima (Susie),

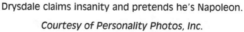

Drysdale claims insanity and pretends he's Napoleon.

Courtesy of Personality Photos, Inc.

The Beverly Hillbillies

Lori Saunders (Betty), Danielle Mardi (Helen), Sumi Haru, Kazuka Sakura, and Miko Mayama (Japanese girls).

269. Lib and Let Lib
Granny and Elly, assured of their equal rights, return to the Clampett mansion. GC: Danielle Mardi (Helen), Miko Mayama (Miko), Fuji (Banzai Sakito).

270. Elly, the Working Girl
Elly May gets a job at Drysdale's Commerce Bank and shacks up with Miss Jane. GC: Danielle Mardi (Helen), Charles Lane (Foster Phinney).

271. Elly, the Secretary
Jethro is in a panic and leaves home when he learns his childhood sweetheart is coming for a visit. He does not know she has become a beauty contest winner. GC: Louellen Aden (Louellen). *Note:* A *real* beauty contest winner, twenty-year-old Louellen Aden won her role in this episode as part of a promotion with CBS affiliate KNOE-TV of Monroe, Louisiana. Aden was then the current "Miss Dogpatch, U.S.A."

272. Love Finds Jane Hathaway
Dick Bremerkamp, a penniless actor, learns the Clampetts are millionaires and uses Miss Jane to get to Elly May. GC: Mike Minor (Dick Bremerkamp), Charles Lane (Foster Phinney).

273. The Clampetts Meet Robert Audubon Getty Crockett
A fortune-hunting young man passes himself off as a descendant of Davy Crockett to marry into the Hillbilly family. GC: Mike Minor (Dick Bremerkamp), Charles Lane (Foster Phinney).

274. Jethro Returns
Jane Hathaway learns her new boyfriend is a fortune-hunter who would like to marry Elly May and her family's millions. GC: Mike Minor (Bremerkamp), Curt Massey (Officer Massey).

Afterword

It has been said that the sincerest form of flattery is imitation. In that case, the Hillbillies have been flattered many times over, in a variety of ways, but mostly via new twists on their well-known theme song. Although technically parodies are illegal unless authorized, the song has enjoyed much success by hundreds of radio station promotions, hucksters, and stand-up

"I'VE HAD IT WITH THE CRIME, GANG WARS, RIOTS, EARTHQUAKES, BRUSH FIRES, MUDSLIDES, HIGH TAXES, AND STATE BUDGET CRISES -- STEP ON IT, JETHRO ... WE'RE GOIN' BACK HOME !! ....."

comics alike. This, more than any other theme, has been rearranged so many times because of its instant recognizability and adaptability.

The theme was put to use, with consent of its lyricist Paul Henning, for a memorable parody on NBC's late-night hit "Saturday Night Live" in the mid-seventies. It was a sketch titled "The Bel-Arabs," which aired at the height of the U.S. oil crisis and starred the cast originals: Gilda Radner, Laraine Newman, John Belushi, and Dan Aykroyd.

"When NBC called and asked to parody the theme song, they read the lyrics and I just couldn't believe it," says Paul Henning. "But it was funny as hell, so I didn't care."

Their opening went like this:

"Come an' listen to m' story 'bout Sheik Ahmed.
Poor Bedouin barely kep' his family fed.
An' then one day he was shootin' at some Jews,
An' up thru the ground come bubblin' ooze.

Oil that is . . . Black gold, Texas tea.
First thing y' know, Ahmed's a billionaire,
Kinfolk said, Ahmed move away from there.
Said, Californy is th' place y' oughta be.
So he loaded up th' jet and flew to Beverly.

Hills that is . . . Swimmin' pool, movie stars . . . Jews!"

The parody, pulled off perfectly by the cast of "Saturday Night Live," was a screaming success. The skit had Aykroyd and Belushi as FBI agents coming to question the Clampetts about their fortune. Laraine Newman played Elly May, and Gilda Radner portrayed a fantastically wild Granny. The whole family spoke Arabic, which added to the humor. The show re-created the opening sequence with the Clampetts riding down a Beverly Hills street in the truck and even re-created the Clampett's mansion foyer to near perfection.

Another travesty of "The Ballad of Jed Clampett" was 1987's "Ballad of Jim & Tammy," which circulated on billboards, frequented Xerox machines, and popped into mailboxes all around the country. This was in response to the famous Jim Bakker/PTL scandal that received tons of publicity.

The theme—author unknown—went like this:

Come an' listen to m' story 'bout a man named Jim.
Poor missionary, couldn't stay away from sin.
An' then one day Tammy was shootin' down some ludes,
An' up from the bed come Jessica Nude.

Sex that is . . . Blackmail, guilty pleas!

Well th' first thing y' know, ol' Jim's a millionaire
Falwell says, "Jim, move away from there."
He said Califor`ny is th' place y' oughta be
So they loaded up the limo and cruised to Beverly.

Pills that is . . . sex tools, gay bars!

Well now it's time to say goodbye to Jim and all his kin,
They're mighty glad you folks keep sendin' money in
You're all invited back next week to this locality
To watch Jerry Falwell take away their keys.

Take your clothes off! Set a spell! Y'all come back now, y' hear?"

Postscript

On a hot summer afternoon, taping of the CBS special, "The Legend of the Beverly Hillbillies" had concluded. It was said that when Jed Clampett left the location, there were tears in his eyes.

Photograph by Steve Cox

About the Author

STEPHEN COX currently lives in the Los Angeles, California, area. He has written for *TV Guide*, the *Los Angeles Times*, *The Hollywood Reporter*, and many midwestern newspapers.

Other books by Cox include *The Munsters*, *The Munchkins Remember the Wizard of Oz and Beyond*, *The Addams Chronicles*, *Here's Johnny!*, *The Hooterville Handbook: A Viewer's Guide to Green Acres*, *The Official Abbott & Costello Scrapbook* (with John Lofflin), and *Here on Gilligan's Isle* (with Russell Johnson). Recently, Cox worked closely with Buddy Ebsen as a researcher and editor for the actor's autobiography, *The Other Side of Oz*, due out in 1993.